KITAB AL-JAMI'

KITAB AL-JAMI'

ON THE SUNNAH, COURTESY, WISDOM, MILITARY EXPEDITIONS AND HISTORY

Abu Muhammad 'Abdullah Ibn Abi Zayd al-Qayrawani

(d. 386 AH)

DIWAN ⊕ PRESS

Classical and Contemporary Books on Islam and Sufism

Copyright 1999 © Abdassamad Clarke

First published in Dhu'l-Hijjah 1419/March 1999 by:
Ta-Ha Publishers Ltd.
This edition Rajab 1442/March 2021 by:
Diwan Press
311 Allerton Road
Bradford
BD15 7HA
UK

email: info@diwanpress.com

By: Ibn Abi Zayd al-Qayrawani
Translated by: Abdassamad Clarke

British Library Cataloguing in Publication Data
al-Qayrawani, Ibn Abi Zayd
The Comprehensive Book
I. Title

ISBN   978-1-908892-71-3 (Paperback)
                          978-1-908892-72-0 (Casebound)

Dedication

This book is dedicated to Shaykh Dr. Abdalqadir as-Sufi who opened the door to Madina in our time as he did with many other doors.

Acknowledgements

My thanks to Dr. Yasin Dutton for his invaluable assistance with many of the difficulties of fiqh and Arabic language.

This book is translated from the edition prepared by Muhammad Abu al-Ajfan and ‘Uthman Bittikh, published by Mu’assasah ar-Risalah in Beirut and al-Maktabah al-‘Aqeeqah in Tunis.

Contents

Chapter 1   1
Sunnahs the opposite of which are innovations, on being led and following, the merits of the Companions and about shunning the people of innovation

Chapter 2   22
The sending of the Prophet ﷺ, his days and life-span, genealogy, description, sons, daughters and wives, and the ten Companions and their genealogies and lives, some history and something about when parts of the shari'ah were revealed

Chapter 3   32
The superiority of Madinah, and some mention of the grave, the mimbar, the mosque and the Ka'bah. Mention of the *sadaqat* of the Prophet ﷺ and the expulsion of the Jews.

Chapter 4   39
Knowledge, the guidance of people of knowledge and their courtesies, and some mention of fatwas

Chapter 5   45
On trials and the corruption of the age, mention of commanding right and forbidding wrong, and mention of some who were tried when doing that. On absolving someone who does one wrong, and concerning a man seeking a post of governance

Chapter 6   52
Supplication, remembrance of Allah, recitation of Qur'an and recitation with melodies, stories, dhikr in mosques, written copies of the Qur'an, the unclear speech of non-Arabs, and gossiping after 'Isha

Chapter 7   67

Silence, withdrawal, humility, intention, modesty and good character. Some mention of worship, admonitions and wisdom

Chapter 8   73

Adornment, conceit, showing-off, pride, lying, backbiting and bad opinion

Chapter 9   79

Scrupulousness, earnings, seeking provision, setting wealth right; mention of sadaqah, abstaining from begging, accepting gifts; concerning whether travellers may eat fruits which they come across or buy from slaves; mention of the properties of administrators; and what is permitted to someone in pressing need

Chapter 10   90

Returning greetings, what constitutes reconciliation, greeting people of the dhimmah, brotherhood for the sake of Allah, the contract whereby a slave purchases his freedom, seeking permission to enter, private conversations, kissing hands, going to excess in honouring husbands and relatives, and old or learned people, treating parents well, and responding to one who sneezes

Chapter 11   99

The fitrah, trimming the moustache, shaving pubic hair, circumcision, tooth-sticks, kohl, dyeing hair and tying it up, henna, cupping and entering public baths

Chapter 12   106

Covering the private parts, what covering is required of women and men, mixing of the sexes in eating together and at the time of sleep, going alone with close relatives and others, and a woman's travelling with someone other than a close relative

Chapter 13   112

Food and drink, washing the hands, and eating with the left hand, drinking standing, and other things on food and drink and responding to invitations, hospitality, the hospitality of the people of the dhimmah. Also skinning an animal that has died of natural causes and using its bones

Chapter 14   118
Clothing, silk, materials woven of mixes of wool and silk, dyed materials, dressing in wool, letting the lower garment hang down and wrapping oneself in only a single piece of cloth, seal-rings, jewellery, gold and silver vessels, wearing sandals, images and sculptures, and mention of the form of the people of the dhimmah

Chapter 15   127
Medicine, cauterisation, treatment, charms, seeking protection, amulets, augury, the [evil] 'eye', the plague, treatment for [possession by] jinn, and the stars (astrology)

Chapter 16   136
Using dogs, hanging talismans and bells on animals, branding animals, castrating animals, studs, snakes and ants, etc.

Chapter 17   140
Treating slaves and animals well, women, protecting one's neighbours, orphans, anticipating a reward from Allah for disasters, mention of daughters, and mention of the meaning of the word *bid'*

Chapter 18   145
Travelling, women travelling, voyaging by sea, and commercial journeys to enemy lands

Chapter 19   149
Names, honorific names, genealogies, and dreams

Chapter 20   153
Poetry, singing and entertainment, backgammon and chess, and racing and archery

Chapter 21   157
The Hijrah, military expeditions and history

Author's Afterword   184
People Mentioned in the Text   186
Further Reading   210
Endnotes   214

CHAPTER 1

SUNNAHS THE OPPOSITE OF WHICH ARE INNOVATIONS, ON BEING LED AND FOLLOWING, THE MERITS OF THE COMPANIONS AND ABOUT SHUNNING THE PEOPLE OF INNOVATION

PRAISE BELONGS to Allah Who encompasses people with His blessings, and Who sent Muhammad as the last of the Messengers by His mercy as a bearer of good news and a warner, inviting to Allah by His permission and as an illuminating lamp. Allah, mighty is He and majestic, guides whomever He loves to guide. He sent him while they were upon the edge of a pit of the Fire and He rescued them by him (Surah Ali 'Imran 103). So he, the blessings of Allah upon him and His *barakahs*, undertook to discharge Allah's right upon him among the slaves until Allah took him back to Him praiseworthily after Allah had perfected and completed His *deen* by him, and he had conveyed the messages of his Lord, made every problem clear, and unveiled every enigma. He left the Book of Allah, mighty is He and majestic, for his nation as a clear light, and his Sunnah as a protecting fortress, and his Companions as a strong rope.

The Book and the Sunnah

The Messenger 🕊 said, "I have left among you two matters which, as long as you hold on to them, you will never go astray: The Book of Allah and the Sunnah of His Prophet."[1]

Bid‘ah – Innovation

He also said 🕊 "You must have my Sunnah and the Sunnah of the *khulafa* who take the right way after me; bite on it with the molar teeth.[2] Beware of newly introduced matters, for every newly introduced matter is an innovation and every innovation is a going astray."

Trials and Sects

He 🕊 warned against trials, erroneous opinions (*ahwa'*),[3] innovations and against the slip of a man of knowledge. He said 🕊 "You will mount up on the sunnahs of those who were before you."[4] He 🕊 described the Khawarij[5] and he declared them, because of their innovation, to be those who pass swiftly through the *deen*.[6] The traditions concerning the Khawarij, the Qadariyyah,[7] the Murji'ah[8] and the Rafidah[9] came consecutively.

The seventy-two groups have branched off from the above-mentioned, those which the Messenger 🕊 warned us against, saying that there would be in his Ummah those who separated themselves off from it.[10]

'Aqidah

The Ummah is unanimous on the following matters of the *deen* and sunnahs, the contrary of which are innovations and error: that Allah, blessed is His name, has the most beautiful names and most exalted attributes and He has never been without any of His attributes. He encompasses in knowledge all of that which He creates before its being brought into being and He creates things by His will. His saying is, *"His command when He wills a thing is only that He says to it 'Be!' and it is."* (Surah Yasin, 81).

His speech is one of His attributes and it is not created and thus perishing, nor is it an attribute of a created being and thus perishing. Allah, mighty is He and majestic, spoke to Musa by His essence and He made him hear His speech, not a speech which subsisted in other-than-Him.

He hears and He sees, and He constricts and expands, and His two hands are widespread, *"and the earth will be in His grasp on the Day of Resurrection and the heavens will be rolled up in His right hand"* (Surat az-Zumar, 64).

He will come on the Day of Resurrection, although He does not [literally] 'come' – and the angels will be rank upon rank (Surat al-Fajr, 24) – in order to review the nations, to take them to account and punish and reward them. He will forgive whomever of the wrongdoers He wishes, and punish whomever of them He wishes.

He is pleased with those who are obedient and He loves those who turn [to Him] in repentance, and He is displeased with whoever rejects Him and He is angry with them, and nothing can withstand His anger.

The Throne and the Footstool

He is above[11] His heavens over His *arsh*[12] apart from His earth, and He is in every place by His knowledge. Allah, glorious is He and exalted, has a Footstool (*Kursi*) as He said, mighty is He and majestic, "*His footstool encompasses the heavens and the earth.*" (Surat al-Baqarah, 255)

Of that which is narrated in the hadith literature is that Allah, glorious is He, will place His Footstool on the Day of Resurrection to decide the judgement.[13]

Mujahid said, "They used to say, 'What are the heavens and the earth compared to the Footstool but like a ring cast in the desert?'"

The Vision of Allah

Allah's close friends will see Him, glorious is He, in the next life with the eyes which are in their faces and they will not be wronged or defrauded with respect to His vision, as He said, mighty is He and majestic, in His Book[14] and upon the tongue of His Prophet. The Messenger ﷺ spoke about His words, glorious is He, "*For the ones who do excellently well there is the best and increase,*" (Surah Yunus, 26). He said, "The best is the Garden and the increase is gazing towards the face of Allah, exalted is He."

Allah will speak to the slaves on the day of Resurrection without there being an interpreter between Him and them.

The Garden and the Fire

The Garden and the Fire have already been created; the Garden is prepared for people of *taqwa* and the Fire for those who cover over [the truth]; neither of them will pass away or perish.

The Decree

One must have Iman in the decree, the good of it and its evil; all of that our Lord has decreed and His knowledge enumerates it. The decreeing of affairs is in His hands, their source is His specific decree. He is gracious to whoever obeys Him and He guides him, makes Iman beloved to him, makes it easy for him, expands his breast for him and guides him, *"and whomever Allah guides is guided."* (Surat al-Isra', 97). He disgraces whoever disobeys and rejects Him, and He forsakes him, eases him to that path, veils him and makes him go astray, and whomever Allah leads astray then you will never find a guide for him (Surat al-Kahf, 16). Everyone comes to that which He already knows and there is no escape from that for anyone.

Iman

Iman is a word on the tongue, sincerity in the heart, and action with the limbs. It increases with obedience and decreases through disobedience with a decrease from the realities of completion and perfection not in a way which invalidates Iman. There is no speech without action, and there is no speech and action without intention, and there is no speech, action and intention without compliance with the Sunnah.

Major Wrong Actions

None of the people of the *qiblah* becomes a *kafir* through a wrong action even if it is a major one, and nothing invalidates Iman except for associating partners with Allah, as He said, glorious is He, *"Definitely if you associate others [with Allah] your action will come to nothing."* (Surat az-Zumar, 65). Allah does not forgive anything being associated as partner with Him, and He forgives apart from that whomever He wishes (See Surat an-Nisa', 48).

Recording Angels

There are guardian recorders [angels] over the slaves writing their actions, as our Lord said, blessed is He and exalted, in His Book (Surat al-Infitar, 10), and nothing of that escapes His knowledge.

Death

The angel of death takes all the spirits by the permission of Allah, as He said, glorious is He, *"Say, 'The angel of death who has been entrusted with you will take you back'."* (Surat as-Sajdah, 11)

People die at their appointed times, and of them there are the spirits of the people of happiness who remain in bliss until the day they are raised up, and the spirits of the people of grief who remain in Sijjin [in the Fire], tormented until the Day of Reckoning.

The Shuhada – Witnesses

The *shuhada'* ('martyrs/witnesses') are alive with their Lord, provided for (Surah Ali 'Imran, ayah 169).

The Grave

The torment of the grave is true. The believers will be tried [by the questioning of Munkar and Nakir] in their graves. They will be squeezed and tested. Allah will strengthen the word of whomever He wishes to strengthen.

The Resurrection

The Trumpet will be blown so that whoever is in the heavens and the earth will lose consciousness except for whomever Allah wills. Then later it will be blown another time, and then they will be there standing gazing; just as He originated them they will return, naked, barefoot and uncircumcised.

The bodies which obeyed and disobeyed are the ones which will be resurrected on the Day of Resurrection in order for them to be recompensed [for their good and bad actions]. The skins which they had in the world are the ones which will bear witness, and the tongues, hands and feet are the ones which will bear witness against them on the Day of Resurrection, against whomever of them they bear witness.

The Scales

The scales will be set up to weigh the slaves' actions. Whoever's scales are heavy will succeed and whoever's scales are light will fail and lose. They will be given their pages [on which are the records of their deeds], and whoever is given his book in his right hand will be taken to account with an easy reckoning. Whoever is given his book in his left hand will roast in a blazing fire.

The Sirat

The Sirat is a bridge to which they will come, over which the slaves cross according to the measure of their actions, so that there are those who are saved – at different speeds of crossing over – from the fire of Jahannam, and there are people whose actions bind them in the Fire. Whoever has any Iman in his heart will come out of the Fire.

Intercession

Intercession will be made for people of great wrong action among the believers. A people from his Ummah will come out of the Fire by the intercession of the Messenger of Allah 🕌 after they have already become charred, then they will be cast into the river of life and will sprout as grain does.

The Basin (*hawd*)

Iman includes belief in the basin of the Messenger of Allah 🕌 to which his Ummah will come to drink. Whoever drinks from it will never thirst again, and whoever changed and altered [the *deen*] will be chased away.

The Night Journey

Iman includes belief in what has been narrated about the Night Journey of the Prophet ﷺ to the heavens according to the authentic narrations, and that he saw the greatest sign of his Lord.[15]

Sayyiduna 'Isa, the Dajjal and the Signs of the Hour

And [Iman] is required in that which is firmly established of the appearance of the Dajjal and the descent of 'Isa ibn Maryam ﷺ and his ['Isa's] killing him [the Dajjal]; and in the signs which will occur before the Hour: the rising of the sun from its place of setting, the appearance of the Beast, etc., of those things about which there are authentic narrations.[16]

The Clear (*muhkamah*) and the Ambivalent (*mutashabihah*)

We affirm that which has come to us from Allah, mighty is He and majestic, in His Book, and that which is firmly established from the Messenger of Allah ﷺ of his news. It requires that one act according to that of it which is clear and unambiguous, and we acknowledge that the explanation of the texts which are ambivalent and allegorical and of every reality which is hidden from us belongs to Allah, glorious is He. Allah knows the interpretation of the allegorical [*ayat*] of His Book. Those firmly established in knowledge say, "*We believe in it, all is from our Lord.*" (Surat Ali 'Imran, 7). Some people say, "*The ones who are firmly established [in knowledge]*" know its problematic parts, but the former is the saying of the people of Madinah, and the Book indicates it.[17]

The Best Generations

The best generations are the generation of the Companions, then the ones who followed them (the Followers), then the ones who followed them (the Followers of the Followers), as the Prophet ﷺ said.[18]

The best of the Ummah after its Prophet is Abu Bakr, then 'Umar, then 'Uthman, then 'Ali. It has also been said, "then 'Uthman and 'Ali", may Allah be pleased with them, and one refrains from preferring one ['Uthman or 'Ali] over the other. That has been narrated from Malik, and he said, "I have never found anyone whom I emulate preferring one of them over the other" and his view was that one should withhold oneself from [asserting a preference] for either of the two of them. The first statement has also been narrated from him, and from Sufyan and others, and it is the saying of the people of hadith. Then after them are the rest of the ten [Companions who were promised the Garden], then the people of Badr of the Muhajirun and then of the Ansar, and then all of his Companions according to [their] emigration, precedence and merit.

Everyone who accompanied him [the Prophet], if only for an hour, or who saw him, if only one time, then by that token he is better than the best of the Followers.

One must refrain from mentioning the Companions of the Messenger of Allah ﷺ except in the best way. They are the people who have most right to have their good qualities made public. One should seek the best excuses for them, and hold the best opinions of them. The Messenger ﷺ said, "Do not harm me in my companions, for by the One in Whose hand is my self! even if any of you were to spend the like of Uhud in gold he would not equal a double cupped handful or a half of any one of them."[19] He also said ﷺ "When my companions are mentioned then restrain yourselves." The people of knowledge say, "They are only to be mentioned in the best way."

Listening to the leaders of the Muslims and obeying them

No one may rise up against anyone who takes command of the Muslims whether with their consent or by force, and then becomes oppressive, whether he is personally good or bad, whether he is unjust or just. One must fight enemies and perform the Hajj along with him. Paying Zakat to him, if he demands it, will discharge one's obligation. One must pray the Jumu'ah and the two 'Eid prayers behind him.

More than one of the people of knowledge and Malik, said, "One must not pray behind any of them who are innovators unless you fear him, and in that case you can pray and there is a disagreement as to whether one must repeat [the prayer later when one is alone]."

Fighting other Muslims and people of the dhimmah

There is no harm in fighting the Khawarij, thieves from among the Muslims, and people of the Dhimmah who oppose you, in defence of your life and property.

The Salaf

One must submit to the sunnahs. They are not to be contradicted by personal opinions nor are they to be opposed by analogical reasoning. That which the right acting first generations interpreted, we take as our interpretation, that which they acted upon we act upon, and that which they abandoned we abandon. We are permitted to grasp hold of that which they grasped hold and to follow them in that which they made clear, and to emulate them in that which they derived [by *ijtihad*] and what they thought [to be correct] concerning events, and that we should not leave their group over that about which they disagreed or its interpretation.

Everything which we have mentioned above is from the words of the people of the Sunnah and the Imams of the people in fiqh and hadith according to what we have explained. All of it is the word of Malik, some of it textually and some of it is well known as his way.

The Sunnah

Malik said, "Umar ibn 'Abd al-'Aziz said, 'The Messenger of Allah ﷺ and the ones who were responsible for affairs after him laid down sunnahs taking hold of which affirms the Book of Allah, makes obedience to Allah complete and makes one strong in the *deen* of Allah. No one may exchange them or alter them, nor investigate that which contradicts them. Whoever models himself on them will be guided, and whoever seeks help through them will be helped. Whoever abandons them and follows anything other than the way of the believers, Allah will entrust him to that which he has turned and roast him in Jahannam and evil it is as a destination'." Malik said, "Umar's determination in that seemed wonderful to me."

'Amal – the Practice – and Hadiths

Malik said, "The practice is more firmly established than hadiths. One whom I emulate said, 'It is distressing that it should be said concerning the like of that, "So-and-so related to me from so-and-so".' Some men of the Followers used to receive hadiths from others and they would say, 'We are not unaware of these, but the practice is contrary to this." Muhammad ibn Abi Bakr ibn Hazm's brother said to him, "Why did you not give judgement according to such-and-such a hadith?" He said, "I did not find people practising it."

An-Nakha'i said, "Even if I had seen the Companions making *wudu'* up to the wrists I would have performed *wudu'* like that although I recite it '*Up to the elbows*' (Surat al-Ma'idah, 7). That is because they cannot be suspected of abandoning sunnahs. They were the masters (*arbab*) of knowledge and the most eager of Allah's people to follow the Messenger of Allah ﷺ. The only one who thinks that of them is someone who has a doubt about his *deen*."

'Abd ar-Rahman ibn Mahdi, "A preceding Sunnah from the Sunnah of the people of Madinah is better than hadith."

Ibn 'Uyaynah said, "Hadith are misleading except to people of fiqh," meaning that others may interpret a thing according to its obvious meaning but it may have an interpretation which derives from another hadith, or it may have an indication which is hidden from one, or it may be a hadith which is abandoned, the reason for that only being comprehended by someone who is very extensive in his knowledge and his fiqh.

Ibn Wahb said, "Every man of hadith who has no imam in fiqh is astray. If Allah had not rescued us by Malik and al-Layth we would have gone astray."

It has been narrated that the Prophet ﷺ said, "There will carry this flag from every succeeding generation its just and equitable ones; they will remove the alterations of the excessively strict, the borrowings of the falsifiers, and the interpretations of the ignorant from it."[20]

Ibn Mas'ud said, "Whoever takes on a Sunnah then let him take the Sunnah of those who have died, those Companions of Muhammad ﷺ. They were the best of this Ummah, the most solicitously considerate for others in their hearts, the deepest of them in knowledge and the least talkative of them. They were a people whom Allah chose for the company of His Prophet and to establish His *deen*. Acknowledge their superiority and follow them in their sayings. Cling to that of their characters and their biographies of which you are able because they were on the straight path."

Malik said, "Umar said, 'Sunnahs have been established for you and obligations obligated upon you, and you have been left with something absolutely clear unless you deviate with people to right and left."

Malik said, "The ways are plainly apparent and the matter is clear."

That man [Ibn 'Umar] said, "I am more afraid for you of that which you do intentionally than I am of mistakes."

Malik said, "Things are only corrupted when their proper stations are exceeded."

Malik said, "This arguing about the *deen* is nothing at all."

'Umar ibn 'Abd al-'Aziz said, "Whoever makes his *deen* a target for altercations will have to change his position a great deal. The limits of the *deen* are clear; it is not an affair in which personal opinion has any standing."

'Umar ibn 'Abd al-'Aziz said, "I am not an innovator, but I am a follower."

Malik said, "It used to be said, 'Do not give someone with a deviant heart authority over your ears, for you do not know what he will teach you.' An Ansari from the people of Madinah heard something from someone who believed in free-will and it attached itself to his heart. He came to his brothers whom he reckoned sincere advisers. When they forbade him he said, 'How is it with that which has attached itself to my heart? If I knew that Allah would be pleased if I threw myself down from this minaret I would do it'."

Malik said, "A man said, 'I have entered into all of these religions (adyan) and I have not seen anything straight'. One of the people of Madinah who was knowledgeable in Kalam [rational study of 'aqidah] said to him, 'I will tell you why that is: because you have no taqwa of Allah, exalted is He. If you had taqwa of Him, He would have made a way out for you'."

Ijtihad and Bid'ah

One of the sayings of the people of the Sunnah is, "Whoever's exercise of independent judgement (ijtihad) leads him into innovation is not excused, because the Khawarij exercised their independent judgement in interpretation and they were not excused since because of their interpretation they left the Companions. He 🐝 named them those who come out of the deen [like the arrow which passes right through an animal], whereas he said that the one who exercises judgement in the rulings [of the shari'ah] will be rewarded even if he makes a mistake."

Al-Qadariyyah – Proponents of Free Will

Malik said, "The people who believe in the doctrine of free-will (al-Qadariyyah) are the worst people. I see them as fickle people of shallow intelligence and innovations because of many *ayat* which are against them. For example there is the word of Allah, mighty is He and majestic, *'The building they built will not cease to be a cause of doubt in their hearts'* (Surat at-Tawbah, 111). There is *'And He revealed to Nuh, "None of your people will believe except for he who has already believed"*,' (Surah Hud, ayah 36). He also said, *'And they will not give birth to any but wicked disbelievers,'* (Surah Nuh, 27), *'You will entice no one to them except for him who is to roast in the Blazing Fire,'* (Surat as-Saffat, 163) and He said, *'but Allah was averse to their setting out so He held them back'* (Surat at-Tawbah, 46). There are many other ayat."

Increase and Decrease in Iman

Malik said, "Iman is speech and action, it increases and decreases." In some narrations from him there is, "Give up speaking about its decrease, and Allah has mentioned its increase in Qur'an." Someone said, "So some of it is better than others?" He said, "Yes."

One of the people of knowledge said, "Malik only hesitated about its decrease in this narration for fear of what it would lead to, i.e. that we should interpret it that it could decrease until it is all gone which would lead to the position of the Khawarij who declare that wrong actions invalidate Iman. His position is that decrease only occurs in that in which increase can occur, i.e. action."

Someone said to Malik, "Should I say, '[I am] a believer, and Allah be praised'? or 'If Allah wills'?" He said, "Say, '[I am] a believer' and do not mix anything other than it with it." Al-Awza'i also said that. Sahnun said about "do not mix anything other than it with it" i.e. "Do not say 'If Allah wills' nor 'There is no power nor strength but by Allah' nor 'And Allah be praised'." Muhammad ibn Sahnun said, "Whoever does not make an exception (by saying 'if Allah wills') and states positively that he is a believer, has replied to your question by stating that he is a believer with Allah. Whoever makes an exception (by saying 'if Allah wills') and does not assert positively about himself, then we say to him, 'You know best what is within yourself, and that of your belief which is concealed from us so tell us about what is hidden within you. If it is like this..." and he mentioned the basic requirements of Iman, "but if it is like this then you are a hypocrite and the like." Those of our Imams who asserted their Iman positively did not mean that they had completed and perfected their Iman, but rather they meant "a wrongdoing believer" saying "I believe in Allah and His Messengers and that which His Messengers brought, so I am a believer in that with Allah at this time and Allah knows best my conclusion."

Malik said, "The [Muslim] people of wrong action are wrong-acting believers."

Action and Iman

Allah, mighty is He and majestic, has named action 'Iman'. He said, *"Allah would not waste your Iman"* (Surat al-Baqarah, 143) meaning, "Your prayer towards the Bait al-Maqdis."

The Qur'an

Malik said, "The Qur'an is the speech of Allah, and His speech does not come to an end or cease and it is not a created thing."

Allah's Establishment on the Throne

A man said to Malik, "Abu 'Abdullah, '*The All-Merciful is established firmly on the Throne*' (Surah Ta Ha, 4), how is He firmly established?" He said, "The firm establishment is not unknown, the how of it is not intelligible, asking about it is an innovation, to believe in it is a duty, and I see that you are a man of innovation; throw him out!"[21]

The Vision of Allah

Someone said to Malik, "Will Allah be seen on the Day of Resurrection?" He said, "Yes. Allah, mighty is He and majestic, says, '*Faces on that day are bright gazing towards their Lord.*' (Surat al-Qiyamah, 23) And He said, mighty is He and majestic, in another ayah, '*No! They on that day are veiled from their Lord*' (Surat al-Muttaffifin, 15)." Malik said, "Abdullah ibn 'Umar said, 'Below Allah there are seventy thousand veils on the Day of Resurrection'."

Narration of Certain Hadiths

Someone said, "What about one who narrates the hadith, 'Allah created Adam on his form,' and that 'Allah will unveil His shank on the Day of Resurrection,' and that 'He will put His hand into Jahannam and bring whomever He wills out of it'," and he [Malik] rejected them strenuously, and forbade anyone to narrate them. Someone said, "Ibn 'Ijlan has narrated it." He said, "He was not one of the people of fiqh." Malik did not reject the hadith of 'descent'[22] nor the hadith of 'laughter'. Someone said, "What about the hadith that 'the Throne shook because of the death of Sa'd'?" He said, "It should not be narrated, and what call has a man to narrate that when he sees what danger it contains?"

Someone said, "What about the hadith, 'Whoever says "Kafir!" to his brother has brought it upon one of the two of them'?" He said, "I think it is about the Haruriyyah."[23] Someone said, "Do you think that they are disbelievers because of that?" He said, "I do not know."

Heretics

Someone said, "Should someone who has the strength talk with heretics, the Ibadiyyah,[24] people of the doctrine of free-will, and people of erroneous opinions?" He said, "No. The Khawarij only took exception to acts of disobedience, but these others talk about the matter of Allah. That man, meaning Ibn 'Umar, said, 'As for me, I am upon a clear way from my Lord. As for you, go to a doubter like yourself and argue with him'."

Malik said, "Do not greet people of erroneous opinions, and do not sit with them unless you are tough with them. Their sick ones should not be visited, and hadiths must not be narrated from them." Malik said, "Luqman said to his son, 'My son, do not sit with the wicked and do not walk with them' and he said, 'Sit with the people of fiqh and walk with them so that if Allah sends down some mercy on them it will happen to you along with them'."

Malik said, "I think that people of erroneous opinions and people of the doctrine of free-will should be sought to repent, then if they repent [well and good] and if not, then they should be fought." Sahnun said, "What I say is that if their dwellings are distinct and they call others to their innovation they must be fought. If their dwellings are not distinct and they call others to their innovation they must not be greeted, nor should they be married, their sick should not be visited and their funerals should not be attended, in order to teach them manners, and they should be disciplined and imprisoned until they turn back from their innovation," meaning, as 'Umar did with Subaigh,[25] "yet their heirs do inherit from them. If they die, even if they had incited people, there is no harm if the prayer is said over them [i.e. they are Muslims]."[26]

CHAPTER 2

THE SENDING OF THE PROPHET 碌, HIS DAYS AND LIFE-SPAN, GENEALOGY, DESCRIPTION, SONS, DAUGHTERS AND WIVES, AND THE TEN COMPANIONS AND THEIR GENEALOGIES AND LIVES, SOME HISTORY AND SOMETHING ABOUT WHEN PARTS OF THE SHARI'AH WERE REVEALED

MORE THAN one of the people of knowledge say, much of which is memorised from Malik, the meaning of which is contained in the following:

The Mawlid and the First Revelation of Qur'an

THE MESSENGER of Allah 碌 was born on Monday after twelve nights had passed of Rabi' al-Awwal in the Year of the Elephant, and he was made a Prophet on a Monday. Malik and others said that he was then forty. Muhammad ibn 'Abdullah ibn 'Abd ar-Rahim al-Barqi said, "Some say that the Qur'an was revealed to him when he was forty-three years old."

Malik said, "He resided in Makkah for ten years [after the revelation] and in Madinah for ten years."

The Salat, Zakat and the Fast

They say, "The prayers were made obligatory as five prayers in Makkah on the Night of the Isra' (the Night Journey from Makkah to Bait al-Maqdis, from where the Mi'raj was made to the heavens), and the Isra' took place in Makkah. The prayer was completed in Madinah. Zakat and the Fast were made obligatory in Madinah."

The Hajj

Malik said, "Abu Bakr established Hajj for people in the ninth year, and the Prophet ﷺ performed Hajj in the tenth year." Some say, "Hajj was made obligatory in the ninth year, but after Abu Bakr had gone to establish the Hajj not as an obligation but in order to re-establish Hajj according to how it had previously been. If it had been obligatory the Messenger of Allah ﷺ would not have delayed it until the tenth year." Those who say, "It was made obligatory in the eighth year," are refuted by that.

The Changing of the Qiblah

Malik said, "The Qiblah was changed two months before Badr."

The Death of the Messenger

They say, "The Messenger of Allah ﷺ died on Monday after twelve nights had passed of Rabi' al-Awwal, when the mid-morning sun was very intense, eleven years after the Hijrah, when he was sixty-three years old, according to what A'ishah and Ibn 'Abbas said." Malik narrated from Anas ibn Malik that he was sixty years old.

Malik said, "The Messenger of Allah 🌸 died when Abu Bakr and 'Umar were sixty years old."

The Description of the Messenger

Malik said, "Anas ibn Malik said, 'The Messenger of Allah 🌸 was neither unusually tall nor short. He was neither extremely white nor dark brown. He had neither short curly hair nor lank straight hair'."

Allah sent him at the beginning of his fortieth year, and took him in death at the beginning of his sixtieth year while there were not yet twenty white hairs on his head.

His Children

They say he died 🌸 leaving only Fatimah 🌸 of his children. He had eight children in all, but some say seven. The males of them were: al-Qasim – and it was through him that he 🌸 received his honorific [Abu-l-Qasim] – at-Tahir, at-Tayyib, and Ibrahim. Some say that at-Tahir was at-Tayyib, and some say that he was 'Abdullah. His daughters were Zaynab, Ruqayyah, Umm Kulthum and Fatimah. All his children were from Khadijah bint Khuwaylid except for Ibrahim who was from Mariyah the Copt. Ibrahim died when he was eighteen months old, and some say sixteen months. All his daughters lived until the time of Islam, became Muslims and emigrated.

Zaynab was married to Abu-l-'As ibn ar-Rabi' to whom the Prophet 🌸 married her before the descent of the revelation upon him. Abu-l-'As, her husband, became a Muslim after she did. She died in 8 AH and Abu-l-'As died in Dhu'l-Hijjah in 12 AH.

As for Ruqayyah and Umm Kulthum, 'Uthman ibn 'Affan married them both. Ruqayyah died during the expedition of the Prophet ﷺ to Badr. Usamah ibn Zayd said, "The Messenger of Allah ﷺ left me with 'Uthman to look after her." Then he married Umm Kulthum after her. Some say that Umm Kulthum died in 9 AH.

'Ali married Fatimah in the second year after the Hijrah. She bore him al-Hasan and al-Hussein. She died six months after the Messenger of Allah ﷺ.

The Wives of the Messenger

The Messenger of Allah ﷺ married fourteen women all of whom were Arabs except for Safiyyah. When the Messenger of Allah ﷺ died he had nine wives: 1. 'Aishah the daughter of Abu Bakr as-Siddiq, 2. Hafsah the daughter of 'Umar ibn al-Khattab, 3. Sawdah bint Zam'ah al-'Amiriyyah, 4. Umm Salamah bint Abi Umayyah ibn al-Mughirah from the tribe of Makhzum, 5. Juwayriyyah who was called Barrah which is more accurate, 6. Umm Habibah bint Abi Sufyan ibn Harb the Umayyad; all of these were from Quraysh. From the tribe of Qays there were: 7. Maimunah bint al-Harith from the clan of Hilal; she was the sister of Umm al-Fadl the wife of al-'Abbas ibn 'Abd al-Muttalib, 8. Zaynab bint Jahsh of the clan of Asad of Khuzaimah, Juwayriyyah bint al-Harith ibn Abi Dirar from Khuza'ah,[1] and 9. Safiyyah bint Huyay ibn Akhtab who was from the Children of Isra'il.

The first of his wives was Khadijah bint Khuwaylid ibn Asad who was from the tribe of Asad of Quraysh. He married her when he was twenty-five years old. She died in Makkah three years before his emigration to Madinah.

He married 'Aishah in Makkah when she was six years old, and some say seven, and she went to live with him when she was nine years old, eight months after his arrival in Madinah. She stayed with him nine years and then he died ﷺ and she lived for forty-eight years after him and died during the month of Ramadan in 58 AH.

His wives who died before him ﷺ were: Khadijah and Zaynab bint Khuzaimah from Hilal.

He did not consummate the marriages with the woman from the tribe of 'Amir nor the woman he married from Kindah before divorcing them.

He divorced al-'Aliyyah bint Dhabyan after he had consummated his marriage with her.

He cohabited with [his slaves] Mariyah the Copt and Raihanah bint Zayd of Bani Quraydhah (a Jewish tribe of Madinah) but later he freed the latter and she rejoined her people. It has been said that he married and later divorced her, and it is also said that she was still his wife when he died.

Ibn Habib said, "One of his wives ﷺ was Fatimah bint ad-Dahhak ibn Sufyan from the clan of Kilab of Qays with whom he consummated marriage."

Those with whom he did not consummate marriages were Mulaykah bint Dawud from the clan of al-Layth, Asma bint al-Harith – and some say she was the woman from the tribe of Kindah – who both sought refuge with Allah from him when they entered in upon him and so he divorced them. There was also a woman from the tribe of Kilab and Layla bint al-Khatim who was from the Ansar.

The Lineage of the Prophet

He was Muhammad ibn 'Abdullah ibn 'Abd al-Muttalib ibn Hashim ibn 'Abd Manaf ibn Qusayy ibn Kilab ibn Murrah ibn Ka'b ibn Lu'ayy ibn Ghalib ibn Fihr ibn Malik ibn an-Nadr ibn Kinanah ibn Khuzaimah ibn Mudrikah ibn Ilyas ibn Mudar ibn Nazar ibn Ma'add ibn 'Adnan.

His mother was Aminah bint Wahb ibn 'Abd Manaf ibn Zuhrah ibn Kilab ibn Murrah.

The Ten Companions Promised the Garden

Abu Bakr as-Siddiq

The name of Abu Bakr as-Siddiq ﷺ was 'Abdullah ibn 'Uthman ibn 'Amir ibn 'Amr ibn Ka'b ibn Sa'd ibn Taym ibn Murrah. It has also been said that he was 'Atiq ibn 'Uthman. Abu Bakr, may Allah show mercy to him, died on Monday eight nights before the end of Jumada al-Akhirah in 13 AH. His khalifate lasted ten nights short of two years and four months.

'Umar ibn al-Khattab

Abu Bakr appointed 'Umar ♒ as the khalifah after him. He was 'Umar ibn al-Khattab ibn Nufayl ibn 'Abd al-'Uzza ibn 'Abdullah ibn Qarat ibn Ribah ibn Razah. He was killed ♒ in Dhu'l-Hijjah in 23 AH. Malik said, "Abu Lu'lu'ah, the Christian slave of al-Mughirah, stabbed him at the time of the morning prayer before he had begun the prayer, and 'Abd ar-Rahman ibn 'Awf led the prayer at his command. Some say that his khalifate lasted ten years, five months and twenty-nine days. Some also say that Abu Bakr and 'Umar both died when they were sixty-three years old. Some say that 'Umar died when he was fifty-five years old. When he was dying he made the appointment of his successor to be a matter for consultation between six people: 'Uthman, 'Ali, Talhah, az-Zubayr, 'Abd ar-Rahman ibn 'Awf and Sa'd ibn Abi Waqqas, and they all agreed on 'Uthman.

'Uthman ibn 'Affan

He was 'Uthman ibn 'Affan ibn Abi'l-'As ibn Umayyah ibn 'Abd Shams whose honorific was Abu 'Amr, and it has also been said that it was Abu 'Abdullah. His khalifate lasted for twelve years, and some say "all but twelve nights". He was killed, may Allah show mercy to him, in 35 AH when he was ninety years old, and some say eighty-eight, and some say eighty-six. He was buried at night and Jubayr ibn Mut'im led the prayer over him.

'Ali ibn Abi Talib

Then 'Ali was pledged allegiance as khalifah. He is 'Ali ibn
Abi Talib ibn 'Abd al-Muttalib ibn Hashim ibn 'Abd Manaf. 'Ali
 took command of Iraq six months after the killing of 'Uthman.
Some say that his khalifate was three months short of five years.
He was struck down on the morning of the Jumu'ah after nineteen
nights of Ramadan. 'Ali died on the night preceding the
Sunday, nine days before the end of Ramadan in 40 AH. He was
fifty-five years old, and some say that he was fifty-eight.

Safinah related from the Prophet that he said, "The khalifate
will be thirty years and then it will be a kingdom." The community
united behind Mu'awiyah in 40 AH.

Talhah ibn 'Ubaydullah

Talhah ibn 'Ubaydullah ibn 'Uthman ibn 'Amr ibn 'Amir ibn
Ka'b ibn Sa'd ibn Tamim ibn Murrah was killed on the Day
of the Camel in the year 36 AH. A stray arrow struck him and
severed the sciatic vein in his leg. He drank a little until he became
exhausted and died. Some say he was seventy-five years old.

'Abd ar-Rahman ibn 'Awf

'Abd ar-Rahman ibn 'Awf ibn 'Abd al-Harith ibn Zuhrah ibn
Kilab. His honorific was Abu Muhammad. He died in Madinah
in 32 AH.

Az-Zubayr ibn al-'Awwam

Az-Zubayr ibn al-'Awwam ibn Khuwaylid ibn Asad ibn 'Abd al-'Uzza ibn Qusayy ibn Kilab. His honorific was Abu 'Abdullah. He was killed in Jumada al-Ula on the Day of the Camel when he was leaving the battle. Some also say that it was in Rajab. It was in 36 AH. Ibn Jarmuz of Bani Tamim killed him. He was sixty-four years old. 'Ali ibn Abi Talib ﷺ said to him [Ibn Jarmuz], "I heard the Messenger of Allah ﷺ saying, 'Give news to the one who kills Safiyyah's son [az-Zubayr] of the Fire'."

Sa'd ibn Abi Waqqas

Abu Waqqas's name was Malik ibn Uhayb ibn 'Abd Manaf ibn Zuhrah ibn Kilab ibn Murrah ibn Ka'b. Sa'd's honorific was Abu Ishaq. He died in 55 AH. Some also say that it was in 56 AH. He was eighty-three years old. Malik said, "He died in al-'Aqiq and was carried to Madinah." Some say that Ibn 'Umar went out to him at al-'Aqiq, which is four miles from Madinah, at the beginning of the day of Jumu'ah, and so he missed the Jumu'ah.

Sa'id ibn Zayd

Sa'id ibn Zayd ibn 'Amr ibn Nufayl ibn 'Abd al-'Uzza ibn Qart ibn Riyah ibn Razah ibn 'Adi. His honorific was Abu-l-A'war. He died in 51 AH. He had come from Sham as the Prophet ﷺ left Badr. The Prophet ﷺ allotted him his portion and his reward (i.e. he was given a share of the booty as if he had been one of those who had fought in the battle).

Abu 'Ubaydah ibn al-Jarrah

His name was 'Amir ibn 'Abdullah ibn al-Jarrah ibn Hilal ibn Ahyab ibn Dabbah ibn al-Harith ibn Fihr. He died in Sham in Jordan in 18 AH.

There is a chapter at the end of the book on history, the Hijrah and the military expeditions.

CHAPTER 3

THE SUPERIORITY OF MADINAH, AND SOME MENTION
OF THE GRAVE, THE MIMBAR, THE MOSQUE AND THE
KA'BAH. MENTION OF THE SADAQAT OF THE PROPHET
AND THE EXPULSION OF THE JEWS.

The Superiority of Madinah

MALIK SAID, "Allah, glorious is He, chose Madinah for the Messenger of Allah for his living and his dying. It was taken as an abode through Iman and Hijrah. All of the cities, even Makkah, were conquered by the sword, and Madinah was conquered by the Qur'an."

Malik said, "When 'Umar turned back at Sar' and looked towards Madinah, he said, 'This is the place of abode'." Malik said, "If 'Umar had known of a place better than it he would not have asked Allah to be buried in it." Malik said, "In it is the grave of the Messenger of Allah , his traces and his mimbar. From it the best of people will be gathered, and the Prophet blessed it, its *mudd* and its *sa'*.[1] He urged them to reside in it and to be patient in its difficulties." It is narrated that he said, "O Allah You have brought me out of the place which is most beloved to me, so make me dwell in the place which is most beloved to You," and He made him dwell in Madinah.

'Umar ibn al-Khattab rejected 'Abdullah ibn 'Abbas's saying Makkah is better than Madinah.

Malik said, "'Umar ibn al-Khattab said, 'The mosque which is founded on taqwa (see Surat at-Tawbah, 108) is the mosque of the Messenger of Allah'."

Malik said, "I have heard that Jibril established its Qiblah for the Prophet 🕮." About the saying of the Prophet 🕮 "A salat in this mosque of mine is better than one thousand *salat*s in any other mosques except for the Masjid al-Haram [in Makkah]" some say that its explanation is that it is superior [to the prayer in the Masjid al-Haram], but by less than a thousand times.

The Mimbar

He said, "That which is between my grave and my mimbar is one of the meadows of the Garden and my mimbar is upon my basin." In another hadith, "Upon one of the mouths of the rivers of the Garden."

Malik said, "I forbade one of the governors from ascending the mimbar of the Messenger of Allah 🕮 in *khuff*s (leather socks) or sandals, and I don't think [he should do] that. Similarly, the qiblah (i.e. at the Ka'bah), and there is no harm in someone putting his sandals in the knot of his waist wrapper or in his belt when he enters the Ka'bah."

He said, "Between the mimbar of the Messenger of Allah 🕮 and the wall of the qiblah there was space enough for the passage of a person walking. Later 'Umar extended it to the limit of the area set aside for the Imam. Later again 'Uthman extended it to where it is today (at the time the author wrote) and the mimbar remained in its place."

Malik said, "A carpenter slave belonging to Sa'd ibn 'Ubadah fashioned it [the mimbar] from the edge of the forest for the Prophet ﷺ." Someone else said, "A slave belonging to an Ansari woman." And some say, "Belonging to al-'Abbas." He made it with three steps.

The Graves of the Prophet ﷺ, Abu Bakr and 'Umar

Someone said to Malik, "How were Abu Bakr and 'Umar in relation to the Messenger of Allah ﷺ during his life?" He said, "As they are in relation to him after his death." Meaning in proximity since they are buried along with him in the house which had been the house of 'A'ishah.

Ibn Wahb narrated from Malik that the place of the grave of the Prophet ﷺ is in the wall which is closest to the *qiblah*, and that Abu Bakr's head is at the feet of the Prophet ﷺ and that 'Umar ibn al-Khattab is behind the back of the Prophet, upon him be blessings and peace, and that there remains space for one more grave.

Some also say that the grave of the Prophet ﷺ in the house is the one which is closest to the qiblah, and Abu Bakr is behind him, his head being towards the shoulders of the Prophet ﷺ and that 'Umar is behind him, his head towards the shoulders of Abu Bakr.

Some also say that Abu Bakr is behind the Prophet ﷺ and that his shelf within the grave passes over or beyond the shelf of the

Prophet's grave 🌸 and that the head of 'Umar is at the feet of Abu Bakr, his feet passing over or beyond the feet of the Prophet 🌸.

The very first statement is more firmly established with the people of knowledge.

Some say that space for one grave remains in the house in which 'Isa ibn Maryam, may Allah bless him and grant him peace and our Prophet, is to be buried, and Allah knows best.

'Umar ibn 'Abd al-'Aziz is the one who made the end of the grave to be defined by a corner, so that the grave of the Prophet 🌸 could not be faced and prayed towards. He did that when the wall of the house fell into ruin. He rebuilt it according to this so that the house came to have five corners.

Greeting the Prophet

Malik said, "A man must greet the Prophet 🌸 when he arrives and when he wants to go out." Someone asked, "Should a man who passes by the grave greet [the Prophet]?" He said, "As he wishes." In a narration of Ibn Nafi' there is [that Malik said], "He should greet him every time he passes, and some people do more than this."

Someone asked, "Are there any of these mosques which should be visited?" He said, "The mosque of Quba'." Someone said, "Other than that?" He said, "I don't know."

Malik was asked on the explanation of the first row, whether it is that which is outside the area demarcated for the Imam?[2] He said, "If the area demarcated for the Imam may only be entered with permission, then the first row is that which is outside it. If it may be entered without permission, then it is that which is closest to the Imam."

The Haram of Madinah

The Prophet ﷺ made a haram (sanctuary) of that which is between the two stony tracts of Madinah and the two of them are also [a part of] the Haram.

Malik said, "Locusts may not be caught in Madinah, but there is no harm in driving them off the date-palms."

It has been said that what is meant by the Haram of Madinah is a distance of twelve miles (bareed) on all sides.

The Ka'bah

Malik said, "When Ibn az-Zubayr rebuilt the Ka'bah he poured perfume in cracks of the building."

Malik said, "I asked the doorkeeper guardians [of the Ka'bah] whether they had been given some provision for their guardianship, and they said, 'No. 'Umar ibn 'Abd al-'Aziz was eager to do that but we refused'." Malik said, "That is better for guardianship." Malik said, "No others should share with them in their guardianship because it is an office from the Messenger of Allah when he gave the keys [of the Ka'bah] to 'Uthman ibn Talhah [on the day of the Opening of Makkah]."

The Expulsion of the Jews

Malik said, "The Prophet ﷺ said, 'Two deens shall not coexist within the Arabian peninsula'." Malik said, "That is Makkah, Madinah, the Yemen and the land of the Arabs." Then 'Umar expelled the people of Najran [in the Yemen]. As for the people of Fadak[3] a treaty had been made with them for a half [of the produce of their land]. Their half was evaluated and he gave them camels, pack-saddles and gold for it, and bought it for the Muslims. He expelled the Jews of Khaybar and they didn't take anything away because they didn't have anything [according to the treaty already made with them]. Malik said, "As for Tayma', their affair is clear. Between us and them there is eleven nights' [journey]. It is not an Arab land. It is a district of Sham. I believe that the Wadi's Jewish inhabitants" meaning Wadi'l-Qura " were left because they did not think that it is a land of the Arabs." As for Egypt, Khurasan and Sham they were not expelled from them because they are non-Arab lands. Whoever is expelled from places other than Madinah which they had been inhabiting, may delay more than three days until they have loaded up. 'Umar imposed three days on them in Madinah because they were only passers-by."[4]

Ibn Shihab said, "Khaybar [was conquered] by force, and some of it by treaty, and most of the Kateebah by force." Malik was asked, "What is the Kateebah?" He said, "The land of Khaybar, which is forty thousand palm trees with their fruits."

The Sadaqat and Awqaf of the Prophet ﷺ

The Amir al-Mu'minin wrote that the Kateebah should be apportioned along with the *sadaqat*[5] of the Prophet ﷺ which they divided among rich and poor. Someone said to Malik, "Do you think that it should be for the rich?" He said, "No, I think it should be shared among the poor." He said, "The [produce from the] *sadaqat* of the Prophet ﷺ was distributed by those responsible for it to whoever came to them, giving preference to the most needy. They didn't give it generally to the tribes, and its funds [for its upkeep] came only from its produce until the Amir al-Muminun came to spend on its upkeep from the *bayt al-mal*. Later he collected its dates and would give them to the tribes, giving them to all of them according to their need, whereas before he had not given to all the people in this way."

The *Awqaf* [endowments] of the Prophet were seven walled gardens of date-palms in Madinah.

CHAPTER 4

KNOWLEDGE, THE GUIDANCE OF PEOPLE OF KNOWLEDGE AND
THEIR COURTESIES, AND SOME MENTION OF FATWAS[1]

The People of Knowledge

THE MESSENGER of Allah ﷺ said, "Allah will not wrest knowledge from people but Allah will remove knowledge with the deaths of people of knowledge. When people of knowledge have gone, people will take ignorant leaders who will be asked and so give fatwa without knowledge, who will go astray and lead others astray."

Malik said, "'Abdullah ibn Salam asked Ka'b al-Ahbar, 'Who are the masters (*arbab*) of knowledge who are worthy of it?' He said, 'Those who act according to their knowledge.' He said, 'You have told the truth.' He said, 'What obliterates it from their breasts after they have known it?' He said, 'Eager desire.' He said, 'You have told the truth'."

Narration of Hadith

Malik said, "There never was an Imam in Madinah who narrated two contradictory hadith." Ashhab said, "He meant that no one narrated anything upon which the practice is not based."

Ibn al-Musayyab said, "I used to travel for nights and days in search of one hadith."

Malik was asked, "Can a part of [the text of] a hadith be brought forward and another part be put back [in the syntax of the hadith] as long as the meaning is the same?" He said, "As for in the words of the Messenger of Allah ﷺ I disapprove of it and that anything should be added to them or taken away from them. Whatever is not his words, I see no harm in it if the meaning is the same."

Someone asked Malik also, "What do you think about a hadith of the Prophet ﷺ to which the [letters] *waw* and *alif* are added and the meaning is the same?" Malik said, "I hope that it will be a small matter."

Someone asked Malik, "Can one take from someone who does not memorise hadiths but who is trustworthy?" He said, "No." It was said, "[What if] he brings his books [containing the hadiths] he has heard?" He said, "They are not to be taken from him. I fear that something could have been added to his books at night."

Ma‘n ibn ‘Isa said, "I heard Malik saying, 'Knowledge must not be taken from four, and may be taken from anybody else: it must not be taken from an innovator who calls others to his innovation, nor from a fool who is open in his folly, nor from one who lies in talking about people even if he tells the truth in the hadiths of the Prophet ﷺ nor from one who does not recognise this affair."

Malik said, "The people of Madinah did not have books. Ibn al-Musayyab died without leaving a book. It has reached me that

Abu so-and-so left a mule-load of books, yet Ibn Shihab had only one book in which was the genealogy of his people."

Someone asked Malik, "What do you think about someone who bases himself upon a hadith which a trustworthy person narrated to him from one of the Companions, do you think it is acceptable?" He said, "No, by Allah! not until he hits upon the truth, and there is only one truth. Two contradictory statements cannot both be correct." The like of this has been narrated from al-Layth [ibn Sa'd].

Fatwas

Malik said, "It was not a part of people's fatwas to say 'This is halal and this is haram', but they used to say, 'I disapprove of this and would not do it myself,' and people used to be content with that." In another place, "They didn't use to say 'halal' nor 'haram' except about that which was [stated to be so] in the Book of Allah, exalted is He."

Malik said, "All that has corrupted people is their finding interpretations for that which they do not know."

Malik said, "A man who narrates everything that he hears is not safe and he will never be an Imam." Malik said, "They clothe the truth with falsity." (see Surat al-Baqarah, 39)

Malik said, "That which is predominant in the people's[2] affair is the clear road. A thing may be good but something else may be stronger."

Malik said, "When you hit the mark there is little talk. When there is a lot of talk then the one who talks will make mistakes."

He said, "It is forbidden to raise one's voice in knowledge and to have a great deal of confused and clamorous talk." He said, "Ibn Hurmuz spoke very little and gave few fatwas, and he was one of those upon whom I love to model myself. He was very insightful in speech and he would refute people of erroneous opinions. He was one of the most knowledgeable people about that on which people disagree." Muhammad ibn 'Ijlan said, "I was never in awe of anyone as I was of Zayd ibn Aslam. Zayd used to say, 'Go and learn how to ask and then come back'."

Some say, "If you sit with a person of knowledge be more eager to listen than talk." Malik said, "How often Ziyad the freed slave of Ibn 'Ayyash used to pass by me and say, 'You must be serious. If those dispensations which your companions allow are true they will not harm you, and if the matter is something else, you will have based yourself on seriousness,' meaning on that which Rabi'ah and Zayd ibn Aslam said."

Malik said, "When you see these affairs about which there are doubts then take hold of the one which is more sure."

Malik said, "Sulayman ibn Yasar was the most knowledgeable person in this city after Sa'id ibn al-Musayyab. When there was a lot of talk, confused discussion and showing off in the mosque he took his sandals and stood up to go."

Much Questioning

Malik said, "I do not like a lot of questions and hadiths. I found the people of this city disapproving of that which is among people today. The first of this Ummah were not the most questioning of people, nor did they have this practice of going deeply [into matters]. The Prophet ﷺ forbade a great deal of questioning, and in another hadith he forbade 'it was said and he said' and much questioning." Malik said, "I do not know whether [the hadith] is about the much questioning [concerning knowledge] which you do, or asking [in the sense] of begging."[3]

Malik used to disapprove of haste in giving fatwas and he would often hesitate over cases. He would often say, "I do not know." He said, "The shield of the man of knowledge is, 'I do not know.' When he forgets it, his vulnerable parts are hit."

Malik said, "One of the things which conquers a man of knowledge is when he answers everyone who questions him." Ibn 'Abbas said, "Whoever answers people on everything about which they ask is mad." Malik was asked about something and he said, "I don't like to reply to something like this. 'Umar ibn al-Khattab was tested with things like these and he left them and would not give an answer about them."

'Abdullah ibn Yazid ibn Hurmuz said, "When a man is appointed as Qadi, Amir or Mufti he ought to ask someone whom he trusts about himself and if he thinks that he is worthy of it he should do it, and if not he should not do it." Malik said, "One of the defects of a qadi is that, if he is removed from his post, he does not return to the gathering in which he was studying."

Reading and Writing Hadiths

Malik said, "There is no harm in a man saying about that which he read out to a person of knowledge, 'he narrated to me', just as you say, 'so-and-so taught me to recite (*aqra'ani*)' whereas it is you who recite to him." Someone asked, "If a man reads out to you and I am present, is it permissible for me to narrate it?" He said, "Yes."

Someone said, "What about someone to whom a man of knowledge says, 'This is my book; take it from me and narrate what is in it'." He said, "I don't think that is permissible and it doesn't please me. They only want to carry away [hadiths]." Ashhab said, "Meaning 'Learning many [hadiths] in a short time (lit. a period of residence)'." Other views have been narrated from Malik. It is also narrated that he said, "I wrote down one hundred of Ibn Shihab's hadiths for Yahya ibn Sa'd and he took them from me without reading them out to me." In another citation there is, "Did you read them out to him or did he read them out to you?" He said, "He had more fiqh than that." Ibn Wahb and other men of knowledge permitted writing. *Munawalah*[4] is stronger than *ijazah*[5] if the writing is authentic.

Malik said, "I never wrote on these tablets." He said, "I said to Ibn Shihab, 'Did you use to write knowledge down?' He said, 'No.' I said, 'Were the hadiths repeated to you?' He said, 'No'.

CHAPTER 5

ON TRIALS AND THE CORRUPTION OF THE AGE, MENTION OF
COMMANDING RIGHT AND FORBIDDING WRONG, AND MENTION
OF SOME WHO WERE TRIED WHEN DOING THAT. ON ABSOLVING
SOMEONE WHO DOES ONE WRONG, AND CONCERNING A MAN
SEEKING A POST OF GOVERNANCE

Trials

MALIK SAID, "The Prophet ﷺ said to 'Abdullah ibn 'Umar, 'How will you be when you remain among the dregs of people whose covenants and trusts are confused, and they disagree and are like this?' and he interlinked his fingers. He said, 'What should I do, Messenger of Allah?' He said, 'You must keep to what you know and beware of what you don't know. You must keep to yourself and beware of their common people'."

Malik said, "I think that 'Umar only supplicated for death as a *shaheed* for himself because he was afraid that he would change due to the trials. He would have loved to live longer in the world."

The Prophet ﷺ said, "There will come a time to people when a man will be a believer in the evening and a disbeliever in the morning and he will be a believer in the morning and a disbeliever in the evening." It was said, "Messenger of Allah, where will the intellects be in that age?" He said, "The intellects of most of the people of that age will have been wrested away."

Abu Hurayrah recited, "*When there comes the help of Allah and the opening and you see mankind entering into the deen of Allah in throngs*" (Surat an-Nasr, 1-2) and he said, "By Him in Whose hand is my self! they entered into it in throngs and they will leave it in many throngs!"

Malik said, "Talhah ibn 'Ubaydullah said, 'I am afraid of the affair when the fools of mankind dominate their people of knowledge'." He said, " Abu-l-Jahm withdrew and left off sitting in the company of people and said, 'I have experienced evil in being close to people'."

Yahya ibn Sa'id said, "When the trial occurred, Muhammad ibn Maslamah and others withdrew, and Muhammad went to live in ar-Rabadhah.[1] People from Iraq came to him urging him [to come and fight], and he showed them his sword which he had broken." The Prophet 🕮 said, "When you see affairs which you deplore, then break your sword on one of the stones of the stony tract, cling to your house, and bite upon your tongue."

Yahya ibn Sa'id said, "The prayer in the mosque of the Prophet 🕮 was only abandoned on three days: the day of 'Uthman's murder and the day of al-Harrah."[2] Malik said, "I have forgotten the third." Muhammad ibn 'Abd al-Hakam said, "It was the day on which Abu Hamzah the Kharijite rose in revolt." Malik said, "On the day of al-Harrah seven hundred of those who had committed the Qur'an to memory were killed." Ibn al-Qasim said, "I am not sure whether or not there were four of the Companions of the Prophet 🕮 among them." Malik said, "It used to be said that whoever meets Allah without having participated in [spilling] the blood of a Muslim will meet Allah with a light back."

Malik said, "When 'Ali appointed the two arbitrators (*hakamayn*), those Khawarij seceded and they said, 'There is no judge (*hakam*) but Allah,' and 'Ali said, 'A true word by which a falsehood is intended'." They were the first rebellious heresy which erupted. They exceeded the limits and declared people to be disbelievers."

Malik said, "Muhammad ibn al-Munkadir and some of his company were beaten because of their commanding the right and forbidding the wrong. Rabi'ah was beaten, his head and beard shaved for something else. Ibn al-Musayyab was beaten and put into short trousers made of coarse rough hair fibres." 'Umar ibn 'Abd al-'Aziz said, "How enviable a man is someone whom no harm has struck because of this matter."

Malik said, "Abu Bakr ibn 'Abd ar-Rahman and 'Ikrimah ibn 'Abd ar-Rahman went to see Ibn al-Musayyab in prison when he had been beaten severely. They said to him, 'Fear Allah! for we are afraid for your blood.' He said, 'Get out! Do you think that I play with my *deen* as you do?'"

Malik said, "One ought not to reside in a land wherein transactions are other than true and in which the first community are cursed. Allah's earth is vast. May Allah bless a slave who comes upon the truth and acts according to it."

Ibn Mas'ud said, "Speak the truth and you will be known for it. Act by it and you will be one of its people."

Commanding the Right and Forbidding the Wrong

Malik said, "People ought to command obedience of Allah, then if they are disobeyed they will be witnesses against those who disobey Him." Someone said to him, "If there is a man who does wrong actions, should another man command him to do right actions if he thinks that he will not obey him, if he is one of those of whom the wrongdoer is not afraid such as a neighbour or a brother?" He said, "There is no harm in that. There are some people who, if others are gently courteous with them, will obey. Allah, mighty is He and majestic, said, '*Speak to him with gentle words*' (Surah Ta Ha, 44)." Someone said to him, "Should a man command the governor or someone else to do right action and forbid him from doing wrong action?" He said, "If he hopes that he will obey him, he may do it." It was said to him, "If he does not hope [for that], does he have ample excuse not to do it?" He said, "I do not know." Someone said to him, "Should he tell his parents to do right actions and forbid them from wrong actions?" He said, "Yes, '*and lower to them the wing of humility, out of mercy*'. (Surat al-Isra', 24.)"

Malik said, "When a matter distressed 'Umar ibn al-Khattab he used to say, 'By Allah, that will not happen as long as I remain, I and Hisham ibn Hakam'."

Malik said, "A donkey which was carrying milk passed by 'Umar and he discarded some of the milk, because he thought there was too much and that it was weighing it down."

Someone asked Malik, "What about matters which occur openly among us, such as a Muslim carrying wine and walking with a young woman conversing with her?" He said, "I would like some people to undertake [to do something about] that." Someone asked, "What if someone is not strong enough without authority, and he [the ruler] comes to him and gives him permission, should a man command and forbid with respect to that?" He said, "If he is strong enough to do that and it is in harmony with the practice of that which he knows well."

Ibn Wahb said, "I heard Malik saying about someone who sees something concerning which the right should be ordered or the wrong forbidden, he said, 'The people of virtue and fiqh disagree about this'." Malik said, "Should everyone who sees something wrong undertake to give command about it?"

Malik said, "I visited 'Abdullah ibn Yazid ibn Hurmuz and he was sitting on a couch by himself. He mentioned all the parts of the shari'ah of Islam and what of it had been pulled to pieces and his tears poured down."

Malik said, "'Abdullah ibn 'Abd ar-Rahman al-Ansari was a right-acting man who would go to the governor upon some matter to advise him on it and would not be gentle with him about it, nor would he withhold anything of the truth in his words with him." Malik said, "Others would fear to be beaten."

Malik said, "Sa'id ibn Jubayr said, 'If a man were only to command the right and forbid the wrong when there was nothing [wrong] in him [in his behaviour], no one would command the right or forbid the wrong'." Malik said, "Who is this one who has nothing [wrong] in him?"

Absolving Those Who Wrong One

Malik said, "Al-Qasim ibn Muhammad would absolve whoever wronged him, and he disapproved of entering into disputation himself. Ibn al-Musayyab would not absolve anyone." Malik was asked about that when it was said to him, "What do you think about the man who dies and he owes you a debt which he is unable to discharge?" He said, "It is better in my view to absolve him, but as for a man who wrongs a man," and in another narration, "who backbites him and defrauds him, then I do not think that [is right]. Allah, mighty is He and majestic, said, *'There is only something against those who wrong people'* (Surat ash-Shura, 42)." In another narration he said, "One of the people used to absolve whoever wronged him and interpret it as a good action worthy [of recompense with] ten the like of it. This is not clear to me and I don't know what it is, because the one who does not pardon will take his right in full."

Refusing an Appointment

Someone said to Malik, "What about the man who is appointed to an office but refuses, and nominates another for the post?" He said, "If he nominates someone who is trustworthy then there is no harm in it." Someone said to Malik, "What about someone who is invited to take up a post but he disapproves of accepting it and he fears that he will be imprisoned or his back whipped or his house demolished?" He said, "Let him be patient under that and let him give up the post. As for someone who fears for his blood then I do not know what is the limit in that case. Perhaps he has ample excuse to accept the post."

CHAPTER 6

SUPPLICATION, REMEMBRANCE OF ALLAH, RECITATION OF
QUR'AN AND RECITATION WITH MELODIES, STORIES, DHIKR
IN MOSQUES, WRITTEN COPIES OF THE QUR'AN, THE UNCLEAR
SPEECH OF NON-ARABS, AND GOSSIPING AFTER 'ISHA

Dhikr of Allah

MALIK SAID, "Mu'adh ibn Jabal said, 'The Adamic person does not do an action more likely to rescue him from the punishment of Allah than remembrance of Allah.'"

Supplication – Morning and evening

It is narrated from the Prophet ﷺ that one of his supplications every morning and evening was:

$$اَللّٰهُمَّ بِكَ نُصْبِحُ وَبِكَ نُمْسِي وَبِكَ نَحْيَا وَبِكَ نَمُوتُ وَإِلَيْكَ النُّشُورُ$$

"O Allah, by You we rise in the morning and by You we come into the evening, by You we live and by You we die and to You is the raising up to life." When it became evening he said: وَإِلَيْكَ الْمَصِيرُ "And to You is ultimate becoming."[1]

اَللَّهُمَّ اجْعَلْنِي مِنْ أَعْظَمِ عِبَادِكَ عِنْدَكَ حَظَّاً وَنَصِيباً مِنْ كُلِّ خَيْرٍ تَقْسِمُهُ فِي هَذَا الْيَوْمِ، وَفِيمَا بَعْدَهُ مِنْ نُورٍ تَهْدِي بِهِ أَوْ رَحْمَةٍ تَنْشُرُهَا أَوْ رِزْقٍ تَبْسُطُهُ أَوْ ذَنْبٍ تَغْفِرُهُ أَوْ شِدَّةٍ تَدْفَعُهَا أَوْ فِتْنَةٍ تَصْرِفُهَا أَوْ مُعَافَاةٍ تَمُنُّ بِهَا، بِرَحْمَتِكَ إِنَّكَ عَلَى كُلِّ شَيْءٍ قَدِيرٌ

"O Allah, make me one of the greatest of Your slaves with You in fortune and in portion, in every good which You apportion this day and afterwards, of light by which You guide or mercy which You spread out or provision which You expand or harm which You remove or wrong action which You forgive or difficulty which You repel or trial which You avert or wellbeing which You grant by Your mercy. Truly You have power over everything."[2]

One of his supplications was:

اَللَّهُمَّ بِنُورِكَ اهْتَدَيْنَا وَبِفَضْلِكَ اسْتَغْنَيْنَا وَفِي كَنَفِكَ أَصْبَحْنَا وَأَمْسَيْنَا

"O Allah, by Your light we are guided, and by Your bounty we seek to be free from want, and in Your protection we get up in the morning and go into the evening."

One of his supplications before sleep was that he would place his right hand under his right cheek and his left hand on his left thigh and then say:

بِاسْمِكَ رَبِّي وَضَعْتُ جَنْبِي وَبِكَ أَرْفَعُهُ، إِنْ أَمْسَكْتَ نَفْسِي
فَارْحَمْهَا وَإِنْ أَرْسَلْتَهَا فَاحْفَظْهَا بِمَا تَحْفَظُ بِهِ عِبَادَكَ الصَّالِحِينَ.
اللّهُمَّ أَسْلَمْتُ وَجْهِي إِلَيْكَ، وَفَوَّضْتُ أَمْرِي إِلَيْكَ، وَأَلْجَأْتُ
ظَهْرِي إِلَيْكَ رَغْبَةً وَرَهْبَةً إِلَيْكَ، لاَ مَلْجَأَ وَلاَ مَنْجَا مِنْكَ إِلاَّ
إِلَيْكَ، آمَنْتُ بِكِتَابِكَ الَّذِي أَنْزَلْتَ، وَبِرَسُولِكَ الَّذِي أَرْسَلْتَ.

"O Allah with Your name I lay my side down and with Your name I will raise it up. O Allah if You withhold my self [in death] then forgive it, and if You send it [and it awakens] then guard it with that with which You guard Your right-acting slaves.[3] O Allah I surrender my self to You and compel my back to have recourse to You, and I hand over my affair to You, and direct my face towards You out of fear of You and desiring You. There is no means of safety and no recourse for protection from You but to You, I seek Your forgiveness and I turn to You. I believe in Your Book which You sent down and in Your Messenger whom You sent."[4] Then he would say:

اللّهُمَّ قِنِي عَذَابَكَ يَوْمَ تَبْعَثُ عِبَادَكَ

"My Lord protect me from Your torment on the day when You resurrect Your slaves,"[5] saying it repeatedly.

54

On leaving the house

One of his supplications ﷺ when he went out of his house was:

اَللَّهُمَّ إِنِّي أَعُوذُ بِكَ أَنْ أَضِلَّ أَوْ أُضَلَّ أَوْ أَزِلَّ أَوْ أُزَلَّ أَوْ أَظْلِمَ
أَوْ أُظْلَمَ أَوْ أَجْهَلَ أَوْ يُجْهَلَ عَلَيَّ

"O Allah I seek refuge with You from straying or being misled, or slipping or being caused to slip, or wronging [anyone] or being wronged, or behaving ignorantly or that anyone should behave ignorantly towards me."[6]

In the chapter on travel there is mention of supplication at the time of travelling.

Dhikr and Supplications in the Prayer

He said ﷺ "As for bowing, then in it exalt Allah. As for prostration, then in it exert yourselves with supplication, for it is worthy that you should be answered."[7] He meant, "For perhaps you will be answered."

Bowing – Ruku'

It is narrated that of his words in bowing there is:

سُبْحَانَ ذِي الْجَبَرُوتِ وَالْمَلَكُوتِ وَالْكِبْرِيَاءِ وَالْعَظَمَةِ

"Glory be to the Possessor of the Jabarut and the Malakut (invisible kingdom) and of greatness and incomparable majesty."[8]

Prostration

He ﷺ was heard saying while he was in prostration at night:

أَعُوذُ بِرِضَاكَ عَنْ سَخَطِكَ وَبِمُعَافَاتِكَ عَنْ عُقُوبَاتِكَ، وَبِكَ

مِنْكَ، لاَ أُحْصِي ثَنَاءً عَلَيْكَ، أَنْتَ كَمَا أَثْنَيْتَ عَلَى نَفْسِكَ

"I seek refuge with Your good pleasure from Your anger,
and with Your pardon from Your punishment, and with
You from You. I cannot enumerate Your praise. You are as
You have praised Yourself."[9]

Dhikr after the Salat

After every salat it is recommended to glorify [with subhan'allah]
thirty-three times, to magnify [with Allahu akbar] thirty-three
times and praise [with al-hamdu lillah] thirty-three times and to
seal the hundred with:

لاَ إِلَهَ إِلاَّ اللهُ وَحْدَهُ لاَ شَرِيكَ لَهُ، لَهُ الْمُلْكُ وَلَهُ الْحَمْدُ، وَهُوَ

عَلَى كُلِّ شَيْءٍ قَدِيرٌ

"There is no god but Allah alone without partner to Him.
His is the kingdom and His is the praise. And He has power
over every thing."

After the Toilet

It is narrated that it is recommended to say after going to the toilet:

الْحَمْدُ لِلهِ الَّذِي رَزَقَنِي لَذَّتَهُ وَأَخْرَجَ عَنِّي مَشَقَّتَهُ وَأَبْقَى فِي جِسْمِي قُوَّتَه

"Praise belongs to Allah Who provided me with its sweetness, and brought that of it which is troublesome out of me, and made its strength remain in my body."

A Supplication

Malik said, "One of the supplications of the Messenger of Allah ﷺ was:

اللَّهُمَّ إِنِّي أَسْأَلُكَ فِعْلَ الْخَيْرَاتِ وَتَرْكَ الْمُنْكَرَاتِ وَحُبَّ الْمَسَاكِينِ، وَإِذَا أَرَدْتَ بِعِبَادِكَ فِتْنَةً فَاقْبِضْنِي إِلَيْكَ غَيْرَ مَفْتُونٍ

"O Allah, I ask You for the doing of right actions, and the giving up of reprehensible actions, and love of the bereft, and when You intend a trial for people that You take me back to You uncorrupted."

Seeking Refuge

The form of seeking refuge which Jibril taught the Messenger of Allah ﷺ when he saw an 'Ifrit [of the Jinn] searching for him with a firebrand on the Isra' (Night Journey) was:

أَعُوذُ بِوَجْهِ اللهِ الْكَرِيمِ وَبِكَلِمَاتِ اللهِ التَّامَّاتِ الَّتِي لاَ يُجَاوِزُهُنَّ

بَرٌّ وَلاَ فَاجِرٌ، وَبِأَسْمَاءِ اللهِ الْحُسْنَى كُلِّهَا مَا عَلِمْتُ مِنْهَا وَمَا لَمْ

أَعْلَمْ مِنْ شَرِّ مَا خَلَقَ وَذَرَأَ وَبَرَأَ، وَمِنْ شَرِّ مَا يَنْزِلُ مِنَ السَّمَاءِ

وَمِنْ شَرِّ مَا يَعْرُجُ فِيهَا، وَمِنْ شَرِّ مَا ذَرَأَ فِي الْأَرْضِ وَمِنْ شَرِّ

مَا يَخْرُجُ مِنْهَا، وَمِنْ فِتْنَةِ اللَّيْلِ وَالنَّهَارِ، وَمِنْ طَوَارِقِ اللَّيْلِ

وَالنَّهَارِ إِلاَّ طَارِقاً يَطْرُقُ بِخَيْرٍ يَا رَحْمَنُ

"I seek refuge with the face of Allah, the Generously Noble, and with the complete words of Allah which neither a wicked nor a good person can pass beyond, from the evil of that which descends from the sky and the evil of what ascends into it, and the evil of what He planted in the land and the evil of what comes out of it, and from the trials of night and day and from events which occur in the night and day except for an event that brings good, O All-Merciful." Malik said, "It used to be said:

أَعُوذُ بِكَ مِنْ جَوْرٍ بَعْدَ كَوْرٍ

"I seek refuge in You from deviating after increase,"
and it is narrated: بَعْدَ طُورٍ "...after a time," which is to change after a good state that one had.

Some say:

أَعُوذُ بِكَ مِنْ جَارِ سَوْءٍ فِي دَارِ مُقَامَةٍ

"I seek refuge with You from an evil neighbour in an eternal abode."

Alighting in a House

Malik said, "The Prophet ﷺ said, 'Whoever alights in a dwelling, let him say:

أَعُوذُ بِكَلِمَاتِ اللهِ التَّامَّاتِ مِنْ شَرِّ مَا خَلَقَ

"I seek refuge with Allah's perfect words from the evil of what He creates," then nothing will harm him until he sets out on his travels again'[10]."

Entering a House

Malik, "It is recommended for a man to say when entering his house:

مَا شَاءَ اللّهُ لاَ قُوَّةَ إِلاَّ بِاللّهِ

'It is what Allah wills! There is no strength but by Allah,' (Surat al-Kahf, 39) and it is in the Book of Allah, mighty is He and majestic."

Supplicating for Death

He said, "'Umar ibn al-Khattab supplicated for his own death when he said, 'O Allah, my years are many, my strength has weakened, and my flock has multiplied, so take me back to You as one who is not neglectful or immoderate'."

He said, "Umar ibn 'Abd al-'Aziz said to one of those with whom he would spend time alone, 'Ask for death for me'. 'Umar ibn 'Abd al-'Aziz used to supplicate:

$$\text{اَللَّهُمَّ رَضِّنِي بِقَضَائِكَ وَأَسْعِدْنِي بِلِقَائِكَ حَتَّى لاَ أُحِبُّ تَأْخِيرَ شَيْءٍ عَجَّلْتَهُ وَلاَ تَعْجِيلَ شَيْءٍ أَخَّرْتَهُ}$$

'O Allah make me content with Your decree and make Me happy with meeting You so that I do not wish for the delay of anything You have hastened nor the hastening of anything You have delayed'."

Raising the Hands in Supplication

Malik said, "Amir ibn 'Abdullah used to raise his hands in supplication after the prayer, and there is no harm in it as long as one does not raise them extremely high." In the narration of Ibn Ghanim, "Raising the hands in supplication is not the way of people of fiqh."

Swearing an Oath

Malik said, "I disapprove of anyone swearing the oath, 'By the right of the seal which is on my mouth!' or that he should say, 'May my pride (literally 'nose') be humbled for Allah'. It has reached me that 'Umar ibn 'Abd al-'Aziz said, 'May my pride be humbled, to Allah belongs the praise, to Allah the One who cut the portion of time [given to] al-Hajjaj'."

After the Morning Prayer

Malik was asked about sleeping after the morning prayer and he said, "Some other time is better than it, but it is not haram."

Malik said, "Sa'id ibn Abi Hind, Nafi' the freed slave of Ibn 'Umar and Musa ibn Maisurah used to sit after the morning prayer until the sun was high, then they would go their separate ways, none of them talking to the other, being occupied in dhikr of Allah, exalted is He."

Reciting Qur'an in the Mosque

"Recitation from a copy of the Qur'an (*mushaf*) in the mosque was not the practice of the very first people. Al-Hajjaj was the first to innovate it. I disapprove of reciting from a copy of the Qur'an in the mosque."

Storytelling in the Mosque

Malik strongly rejected the telling of stories in the mosque. Tamim ad-Dari said to 'Umar, "Let me supplicate Allah, tell stories and mention Allah." 'Umar said, "No." So he asked him again. 'Umar said, "You want to say, 'I am Tamim ad-Dari, so know me!'"

Malik said, "I don't think that anyone should sit with them. Storytelling is an innovation." He said, "People do not need to face them as they face one who gives the khutbah. Ibn al-Musayyab and others used to hold their circles at the same time as the storytellers told their tales."

Malik said, "I forbade Abu Qudamah from standing after the prayer and saying, 'Do such-and-such'." He disapproved also of the box placed in the mosque for sadaqah.

Eating in the Mosque

Malik was asked about eating in the mosque and he said, "As for little things such as a gruel of parched barley or little amounts of food I hope [that it is acceptable], but if one were to go out to the door of the mosque it would be preferable to me. As for much [food] it does not please me not even in the courtyard. I disapprove of the fans which are in the front part of the mosque with which people fan themselves." He said about someone eating meat in the mosque, "Does he not go out to wash his hands?" They said, "Of course." He said, "Then let him go out to eat anything like this."

The Mosque in General

Malik said, "I disapprove of talking in the languages of non-Arabs in the mosque. I disapprove of someone who builds a mosque taking a residence on top of it in which to live with his family. One should not clip one's nails in the mosque, nor cut one's moustache even if one takes [the hairs or nails] away in one's robe. I disapprove of using the *miswak* (the toothstick) in the mosque because of what comes off the *miswak* from the mouth which one then discards [in the mosque]. I do not like rinsing out the mouth in the mosque. One should go out to do that." He disapproved of people gathering to eat food in the mosque in Ramadan.

He was asked about the use made of mosques in villages which are used for children to eat and spend the night in. He said, "I hope that it is a light matter."

The Qur'an

Malik said, "If you are able to make the Qur'an an Imam then do it, for it is the one which leads to the Garden." Someone asked, "What about the man who retains and understands it and who concludes [the recitation of Qur'an] in a night?" He said, "How excellent that is!" Someone asked, "Should one recite on the roadway." He said, "Some small amount. As for one who does that perpetually, no." Sahnun said, "There is no harm in a rider and someone reclining in order to sleep reciting Qur'an." Someone asked, "What about a man who goes walking to his town, may he recite?" He said, "Yes." Someone asked, "If he goes to a market, may he recite within himself as he walks." He said, "I disapprove of reciting in the market."

He was asked about reciting in public baths and he said, "Public baths are not places for recitation, but if someone recites some ayats there is no harm in that."

He was asked about a seven year old boy memorising the entire Qur'an and said, "I do not think that this is fitting."

He said, "*An-Nabr* (raising the voice from a low to a high pitch) and the use of hamzah[11] in recitation do not please me." Malik said, "The Qur'an was sent down in seven modes, so recite that which is easy of it."

Singing the Qur'an with melodies

Malik said, "Recitation with modulated tones (i.e. melodies) does not please me, and I do not like it whether in or out of Ramadan because it resembles singing and one is laughing at the Qur'an. People say, 'So-and-so is a better reciter than so-and-so.' It has reached me that slave girls are being taught that in the same way as they are taught singing. Do you think that this is anything to do with the way in which the Messenger of Allah ﷺ used to recite?"[12]

The Writing of the Qur'an

Malik said, "There is no harm in decorating a written copy of the Qur'an. I have a copy which my grandfather wrote, when 'Uthman ﷺ wrote the first copies, upon which there is a lot of silver." Someone asked, "Should the number of ayats be written at the beginning of a surah?" He disapproved of that in source and reference copies, and he also disapproved of vowelling and writing the diacritical points, but as for those copies from which children learn, then there is no harm in writing diacritical points and vowel markings.[13]

Someone asked, "What about those copies written today, should they be written according to what people have decided upon of orthographic usage?" He said, "No, but according to the first writing. The explanation of that is that *Bismi-llahi-r-Rahmani-r-Rahim* is not at the beginning of [Surah] Bara'ah (at-Tawbah), and so it is left out."[14]

The Order of the Surahs

Someone asked, "How is it that the larger surahs are placed first, and yet some of them were revealed before others?" He said, "Yes. But I think that they composed it according to what they had heard from the recitation of the Messenger of Allah ﷺ."

The Basmalah

Someone asked, "Should *Bismi-llahi-r-Rahmani-r-Rahim* be written at the beginning of a surah on the tablets in which they learn, and [at the beginning] of everything they write?" He said, "Yes."

He disapproved of marking ten [ayats] in the written copy of Qur'an with red and the like, and he said, "They should mark tens with ink." We saw Malik's copy of Qur'an wrapped in pieces of silk brocade over which was a red Ta'ifi covering. Malik said, "This is from the brocade of the Ka'bah (the *Kiswah*) and I think that it is a small matter to buy some of it [to cover] a written copy of the Qur'an." He said, "It should not be ornamented with any gold."

Talking after 'Isha

Ibn al-Musayyab said, "That I should sleep through the later 'Isha (i.e. Salat al-'Isha) is preferable to me than that I should talk uselessly after it." Some say that if one talks after it for a bit about knowledge or manual work and the like, then it is not disapproved.

The Names of 'Isha and of the Days of 'Eid al-Adha

Malik disapproved of saying *Salat al-'Atamah* (a term for Salat al-'Isha) and *Ayyam at-Tashriq* (a term for the days of 'Eid al-Adha). He said, "Allah, glorious is He, says, '*And after Salat al-'Isha*' (Surat an-Nur, 58) and He says, mighty is He and majestic, "*And remember Allah in numbered days*" (Surat al-Baqarah, 208)[15] and "*let them remember Allah during known days*" (Surat al-Hajj, 28)[16]

CHAPTER 7

SILENCE, WITHDRAWAL, HUMILITY, INTENTION, MODESTY AND
GOOD CHARACTER. SOME MENTION OF WORSHIP, ADMONITIONS
AND WISDOM

Speech and Silence

MALIK SAID, "The Messenger of Allah ﷺ said, 'A man says a word which earns the displeasure of Allah to which he gives no thought and by which he falls in the Fire of Jahannam'[1]."

He said, "Whoever is protected from the mischief of two [things] will enter the Garden: that which is between his jawbones and that which is between his legs."[2]

He said, "The people with most mistakes on the Day of Resurrection will be those who plunged most into falsehood."

He said, "The person of taqwa is bridled; he does not talk about everything he wants."

He said, "A part of the excellence of a man's Islam is his giving up what does not concern him."[3]

'Isa ibn Maryam, may Allah bless our Prophet and him, said, "Do not speak much without remembrance of Allah so that your hearts become hard, because a hard heart is far from Allah, exalted is He."[4] Malik said, "Whoever does not reckon his speech as part of his action will talk a great deal." Some say, "Whoever knows that his speech is part of his action speaks little." Malik said, "They didn't use to talk as much as this. Some people talk a month's talk in an hour," or as he said. Malik said, "Ar-Rabi' ibn Khuthaim was one of the people who spoke least."

Good Character

The Prophet ﷺ said, "A man attains by his good character the rank of the one who fasts [optional fasts] and stands [in prayer during the night]."

He said ﷺ "I jest, and [yet] I only say what is true."

He said ﷺ "Every *deen* has a character and the character of Islam is modesty."[5]

He said ﷺ "Modesty is a part of Iman."[6]

He said ﷺ to Mu'adh ibn Jabal, "Make your character towards people good, Mu'adh ibn Jabal."[7]

He said ﷺ to the one who asked him to counsel him in a concise manner, "Do not become angry!"[8] He said ﷺ "A strong man is not a wrestler who continually throws his opponents down, but a strong man is one who masters himself upon becoming angry."[9] Sufyan said, "Show true affection to whomever you will, then make him angry and he will afflict you with a tremendous misfortune which will prevent you from living."

Some say, "No one swallows anything better than his anger." Malik said, "Coarse rude behaviour is disapproved. Allah, glorious is He, says, *'If you had been coarse or hardhearted they would have dispersed from around you.'*"[10]

Malik said, "I heard one of the people of knowledge saying, 'Nothing enters into anyone's *deen* which is more serious for him than his being given more time in the world which he uses to no benefit for the next life'." (A reference to Surat Ali-'Imran, 178)

Malik said, "There is nothing of which there is less among people than fairness."

'Aisha &, said, "If people had been forbidden blazing coals, someone would have said 'if only I could taste it'."

Malik said, "Umar said, 'A man's clumsiness is more serious to me than his poverty, because he may gain wealth, but nothing can withstand clumsiness'."

'Umar said, "Do not keep company with someone who deviates [from the right way], and do not disclose your secret to him, and seek counsel about your affair from those who fear Allah."

He said, "A man stood before Luqman and said, 'Are you the slave of Bani al-Hashas?' He said, 'Yes.' He said, 'Are you the shepherd of the sheep?' He said, 'Are you the black man?' He said, 'As for my being black, that is obvious. What is it about my affair that astonishes you?' He said, 'People's treading upon your carpet, their crowding around your door and their pleasure with your words.' He said, 'Nephew, if you do what I tell you, you will be like that'."

Luqman mentioned, "My lowering my gaze, restraining my tongue, the abstinence of my manner of eating, guarding my private parts, fulfilling my pledges, honouring my guest, protecting my neighbour, and abandoning what does not concern me."

Malik said, "Sa'd ibn 'Ubadah said, 'Pray the prayer of a man who is saying farewell as if he is not returning. Despair of what people own because that [despair] is wealth. Beware of covetousness and searching for necessities because that is abiding poverty. You know that there must be words with Allah so beware of that for which you will have to make excuses."

Malik said, "Some say that trial is appointed as a watcher over speech, and that whoever talks and debates a lot with people, his light departs."

Provision and Doing Without (*zuhd*)

Malik said, "At the time of Salim ibn 'Abdullah there was no one, in the manner of doing-without and moderation, who more resembled those who had gone before. He used to dress in a robe which cost two dirhams, and he used to buy a small quantity of dates, and he would himself go to the market for his own needs. Al-Qasim, however, used to dress in *khazz* (a material woven of silk and wool) and in beautiful clothing. Ibn al-Musayyab used to fast uninterruptedly (i.e. every day)." Someone asked Malik, "What is narrated about that?" He said, "The Prophet ﷺ used to do some things to make things easier for people, and a group of the Companions used to [fast] uninterruptedly."

The Messenger ﷺ said, "For he whose concern is the world, Allah puts his poverty right in front of his eyes, disperses his affairs and none of it will come to him except what is decreed for him. For he whose concern is the next life, Allah will enrich his heart, unite his affairs and the world will come to him in spite of itself."[11]

As-Siddiq said, "The world is accursed, accursed is that which is in it except whatever there is of remembrance of Allah or whatever leads to remembrance of Allah."

One of the people of right action said, "Doing-without (*zuhd*) is abandoning that which is haram and the surplus of the halal, and giving up having a position in people's eyes." The words "abandoning what is haram" did not please Sahnun and he said, "It is obligatory to abandon what is haram." He also said, "A part of doing-without is giving up surplus after having had the power to obtain it. There is no good in love of position." Ibn Shihab said, "The zahid (person who does-without/is abstinent) is he whose patience is not overwhelmed by that which is haram [so that he succumbs to it] and whose gratitude is not occupied with that which is halal [so that he fails to thank Allah for His blessings]." In another place someone said to Ibn Shihab, "Who is the forgetful one?" He said, "The one whose patience is overwhelmed by that which is haram and whose gratitude is occupied with that which is halal." Sahnun said, "The doing-without of the wealthy person is his giving it up. The doing-without of the poor person is by intention. Giving up the world by doing-without is better than seeking it and spending it to good purpose." It is narrated that the Prophet ﷺ said, "How often a dusty, dishevelled possessor of two worn-out old garments is not regarded, and if he were to swear an oath by Allah He would definitely fulfil it."[12]

It is narrated that he ﷺ said to 'Abdullah ibn 'Umar, "Worship Allah as if you see Him, and be in the world as if you were a stranger or someone traversing a way."[13]

Humility and Modesty

He said, "Every Adamic person (human being) has a wisdom in his head in the hand of an angel, so that whenever he exalts himself it strikes him with it and says, 'Lower yourself, may Allah humble you!' and whenever he humbles himself for the sake of Allah it raises him up by it and says, 'Rise, may Allah raise you up'."

He said ﷺ "People, be modest before Allah with real modesty!" A man said, "Are we not modest, Messenger of Allah? Are we not modest before Allah?" He said, "Whoever is modest before Allah, let him spend the night with his appointed term before his eyes. Let him guard his head and what it collects, and his belly and what it contains. Let him remember the grave and the testing. Whoever loves the next life, then let him give up the ornamentation of the life of the world."[14]

CHAPTER 8

ADORNMENT, CONCEIT, SHOWING-OFF, PRIDE, LYING, BACKBITING AND BAD OPINION

Pride

MALIK SAID, "A man said to the Messenger of Allah ﷺ, 'I like my clothes to be clean and the thong of my sandal to be two-coloured; is that pride?' He said, 'No. Pride is only [the case of] someone who is foolishly ignorant of the truth and looks down on people'."

He said ﷺ "When you hear a man saying, 'People are ruined,' then he is the most ruined of them."[1] Malik said, "Someone who says it as an expression of sorrow is not the one who is meant. The one who is disapproved of is only the one who says it as an attack and finding fault." Malik said, "I came upon people and they would say, 'The people have gone'."

Malik said, "A man went to see 'Umar ibn 'Abd al-'Aziz and 'Umar asked him, 'Who is the leading man (*Sayyid*) of your people?' and he said to him, 'I am.' He said to him, 'If you were their leading man you would not have said it'."

'Umar said, "Praise is slaughter."

Shirk – Ascribing Partners with Allah

It is narrated that the Prophet ﷺ said, "Allah, glorious is He, will say on the Day of Resurrection, 'Whoever did an action in which he associated another, then it is for him, and I am quit of him. I am the most independent of partners from ascription of partnership."

The Mark of Prostration

Malik said, "Sa'd ibn Abi Waqqas saw a man between whose eyes was a mark of prostration and he said to him, 'How long have you been a Muslim?' The man mentioned to him something of his story in a way which suggested that it was very recent. Sa'd said to him, 'I became a Muslim at such-and-such a time and there is nothing between my eyes'."

Riya' – Showing-off

Malik mentioned moderation (*qasd*) and its virtue, and he said, "But beware of that moderation for which you would like to be honoured and by which you wish to astonish people."

Someone asked Malik about someone who performed the salat for the sake of Allah and then it occurred to him that he would like to be known for it, and that he would like to be met on the way to the mosque? He said, "If the beginning of it is for the sake of Allah then there is no harm. How often that comes from Shaytan trying to prevent the salat."

Man loves to be right-acting. When the Prophet ﷺ asked about the tree which he struck as a simile for the believers, he ['Abdullah ibn 'Umar] said, "I said within myself that it is the date-palm, but I did not speak up and say it." 'Umar said, "I would have liked if you had said it so much more than such-and-such." This will be in the heart that does not possess. Allah, glorious is He, said, *"I cast upon you love from Me."* (Surah Ta Ha, 39)

Ibn 'Umar said, "O Allah make me one of the Imams of the people of taqwa."

Abu Hazim said, "That which is within yourself, and your self is pleased with it for itself, then it is from your self and so fight it. That which comes from your self, and your self dislikes it for itself, then it is from Shaytan, so seek refuge with Allah from it."

One of the people of knowledge said, "Showing-off is that you do an action wanting people to recognise you for it and praise you for it. If your heart accepts this then it is showing-off." Some say that, "Whoever fears showing-off is safe from it." Some say, "A part of good action is that you should not give up a good action for fear of showing-off."

A part of conceit is your seeing yourself having some superiority over people and you hate them and do not hate yourself.

One of the first generations said, "If you are in the *salat* and Shaytan says to you, 'You are showing off,' then increase your prayer in length, for he is a liar."

Malik said, "Conceal all optional extra acts, the salat and others, for that is better."

Truthfulness and Lying

Malik said, "I have heard that a totally truthful man does not become senile." Ibn Mas'ud said, "There is no worse characteristic in a man than lying." Someone asked Malik, "Should a man discipline his family and children because of their swearing false oaths?" He said, "Yes."

'Umar ibn al-Khattab said, "Do not look at anyone's fasting nor his salat, but look to see whether he tells the truth when he talks and if he fulfils the trust when he is trusted, and whether he is cautious at the moment of giving or receiving a trust or a deposit."

Malik said, "The good was not recognised in 'Umar nor in his son 'Abdullah until they spoke or acted." Al-Qasim said, "I came upon people at a time when they were not impressed with words." Malik said, "He meant that only action should be considered."

It is narrated that the Prophet ﷺ said, "Conspiracy, treachery and deceit are in the Fire."[2]

He said ﷺ, "One of the worst people is a two-faced person who comes to these with one face and then comes to these with another face."[3]

He said ﷺ, "One of the worst people is someone whom people protect themselves against because of his evil."[4]

Malik said, "Al-Qasim said, 'There are men whose defects are not mentioned'."

Backbiting

It is related that he ﷺ said, "Backbiting is when you mention something about a man which he would dislike to hear." Someone asked, "Messenger of Allah, even if it is true?" He said, "If you speak a falsehood that is slander."[5]

In one hadith there is that "Whoever removes the robe of modesty then it is not backbiting [to talk about him] in that case." Some say that it means whoever does something reprehensible openly, and Allah knows best. Some say that it is not backbiting [to talk against] a tyrannical Amir, nor about an innovator who invites others to his innovation, nor one about whom others seek one's advice concerning a marriage or his testimony [before a qadi], etc. The Prophet ﷺ said to Fatimah bint Qays about those who had proposed to her, "Mu'awiyah is poor, he has no property."[6]

Similarly, the Imams think that someone of the eminent people whose word is accepted should make clear the affair of whomever it is feared might be taken as an imam and should mention those things about him such as his lying, etc., those things which oblige one to give up narrating from him. Ash-Shu'bah used to say, "Let us sit and backbite for the sake of Allah."

Good Opinion and Suspicion

'Umar ibn al-Khattab said, "It is not permissible for a Muslim man who hears a word from his brother to think evil of it as long as he can find a good explanation for it." Ibn 'Umar was alone with his slave girl and some men saw him, so he brought her to them and said, "She is my slave girl." They said, "May Allah forgive you! Does anyone suspect you?" He said, "No, but I want you to know."

Al-Qasim said, "Truly, I give up something I need from a place, fearing that I might be suspected of some evil."

CHAPTER 9

SCRUPULOUSNESS, EARNINGS, SEEKING PROVISION, SETTING
WEALTH RIGHT; MENTION OF SADAQAH, ABSTAINING FROM
BEGGING, ACCEPTING GIFTS; CONCERNING WHETHER TRAVELLERS
MAY EAT FRUITS WHICH THEY COME ACROSS OR BUY FROM
SLAVES; MENTION OF THE PROPERTIES OF ADMINISTRATORS;
AND WHAT IS PERMITTED TO SOMEONE IN PRESSING NEED

Earnings and livelihoods

AISHAH SAID 🌸, "I said, 'Messenger of Allah, who is the believer?' He said, 'The one who when he goes out in the evening, wonders where his loaf of bread will come from, and when he rises in the morning, wonders where his loaf of bread will come from.' 'Aishah said, 'If people knew that they had been made responsible for the knowledge of, they would undertake that responsibility.' He said, upon him blessings and peace, 'They know that but they collect their livelihoods without any consideration,' meaning, 'They journey without direction'."

'Umar looked at those praying and said, "The great number of times any of you raises and lowers his head does not deceive me. The [real] *deen* is being cautious and meticulous in the *deen* of

Allah, and refraining from what Allah has forbidden, and acting according to what Allah permits and forbids."

It is narrated that he said ⌖ "Whoever begins the evening weak from seeking the halal, will spend the night forgiven."

Al-Hasan said, "There are two types of dhikr: dhikr with the tongue and that is good, and dhikr of Allah with respect to His command and His prohibition is better than it."

Ibn 'Umar said, "Truly, I love to put a screen of the halal between me and the haram without considering it haram."[1]

Seeking Halal Provision

'Umar said, "Whoever has some land let him cultivate it, and whoever has property let him manage it, because a time will soon come when people will only give to those they love."

'Umar said, "I prefer to die upon my camel's saddle seeking the bounty of Allah than to die in my bed."

Malik said, "Ibn 'Umar and Salim [ibn 'Abdullah ibn 'Umar] used to go out to the market and sit in it. Ibn al-Musayyab used to sit with the people of 'abayahs (striped cloaks)."

Malik said, "The correct position is that markets should be at the beginning of the day not at the end of it, as the people of Iraq do."

Giving

The Messenger said ⌖ "The hand which is uppermost is better than the hand which is undermost. Begin [giving] to those for whose sustenance and expenses you are responsible."

Abstinence

He said ﷺ "Whoever abstains [from what is haram and from begging] Allah will help to be abstinent. Whoever seeks to be independent, Allah will make independent. Whoever constrains himself to be patient, Allah will make patient. No one has been given a gift which is better and more encompassing than patience." (*"Only the patient will be paid their wages in full without any reckoning."* Surat az-Zumar, 11.)

'Umar ibn al-Khattab ﷺ said, "Messenger of Allah, did you not tell us that it is best for us not to take anything from anybody?" He said, "That only refers to asking. As for whatever comes without asking, it is only provision which Allah has provided."[2]

He said, "That one of you take his rope and gather firewood is better for him than coming to a man whom Allah has given of His bounty and asking him, and then he either gives him or refuses him."[3]

Sadaqah and Gifts

He, upon him blessings and peace, used to answer invitations and accept gifts, and he would not eat sadaqah. He said, upon him blessings and peace, "Sadaqah is not permitted to the family of Muhammad."[4] Ibn al-Qasim said, "This refers to obligatory zakat. This does not apply to optional sadaqah."

He said, upon him blessings and peace, "Let none of you women despise to [give to] her neighbour, even if it should only be a roasted trotter."[5]

Some say, "The reward of sadaqah given to near relatives is doubled."[6] Malik said, "Sadaqah given to one's relatives is better than freeing slaves." It is narrated that the Prophet said ﷺ "Your sister and your brother, and the nearest to you, then the nearest to you."

He said, upon him blessings and peace, "Give gifts to each other because gifts drive away rancour."[7]

Ibn 'Umar said, "We used to be such that none of us had more right to his dinar than his brother Muslim did. Then that went and there was equal sharing. Then that went and there were loans. Then loans went and backbiting came."

Malik said, "There were eminent people of worship in our city who would return gifts which they were given." Someone asked, "Is there a dispensation in the hadith, 'That which you are given without asking for is only a provision with which Allah has provided you'?" He said, "Yes." Someone asked, "What about one who is given something and there is a condition attached to it?" He said, "I prefer that he give it up if he has no need of it, unless he is afraid of hunger for himself and is in need, then I see no harm." Someone asked, "What about a man of some standing who attends the market and traffics with that thing in a profit-sharing transaction because of his standing?" He said, "There is no harm in that. Ibn 'Umar and Salim used to go out to the market and sit in it."

Malik was asked about the meaning of the hadith concerning squandering wealth[8] and he said, "Preventing it from being spent on its due and putting it to something other than its right use. Allah, glorious is He, says, 'Do not squander' (Surat al-Isra, 26)."

Eating from Other's Property

Someone asked Malik, "What about fruits which have been cut and then left, and there is something [perhaps a bruise or an imperfection] in them?" He said, "If he knows that they (the owners) are contented with his taking it then he may take it." Concerning crops which have been harvested, and there remain some ears [of corn] and something which its owners leave, Ashhab narrated that he said, "He must only eat that which he knows is halal." It used to be said, "Leave that which causes you doubt for that which causes you no doubt."[9] He said, "He should not pasture on the clover unless he knows that its owner permits it." Someone asked, "[What if] he sees him?" He said, "I do not like it unless he gives permission. It is quite likely that he could be shy of him or afraid of him."

Someone asked Malik, "What about a traveller who finds some fruits?" He said, "If it is because of a pressing necessity [then he may eat them] but if not then he may not. The Prophet ﷺ said, 'Let none of you milk anyone else's milking animal without his permission,'[10] and yet he could milk in the morning and the milk would return [to the udder] in the evening, whereas fruit will not return until the next year."

Someone asked, "What about a garden without walls, may a traveller eat from it?" He said, "No." Someone asked, "What about that which has fallen on the ground?" and he disapproved of it and said, "The place dates are put to dry in the sun is on the ground."

Malik said, "There is no harm in harvesting and cutting [fruit] at night." Al-Layth said, "The only reason for its prohibition is because if it is done in the daytime the poor get a chance to obtain some of it."

Someone asked, "Can one eat from one's father's, mother's and brother's gardens if one passes by them?" He said, "No, not without permission."

Someone asked, "What about if the guardian of the orchard gives me something to eat or sells me some food?" He said, "If you know that they have given him permission to do so." Someone said, "How would I know [that]?" He said, "The orchard people tell you that they saw him selling and refusing [to sell], and thus he is like someone who is responsible for sheep and there is no harm in buying from him. As for the slave who [sells] in a clandestine manner, there is no good in it."

Buying from slaves

Someone asked, "What about a slave-woman who comes to one at a watering-place with milk or dates, can one buy them?" He said, "There is no harm if it is not a regular affair. These are the types of things which slaves sell." Al-Layth was asked about when a slave gives hospitality. He said, "I hope that there is no harm in it." Someone asked Ibn al-Qasim, "What about a slave who gives the amount of a dirham or two as a gift and one requites him for it?" He said, "If his owner is not angry with him then there is no harm."

Finding fruit

Malik was asked about a man entering walled gardens and finding dates which had fallen, and he said, "He should not eat any of them unless he knows that their owner is contented with that, except if he is in need, then I hope [that there is no harm]." Malik said, "As for trees in the desert then let him eat whatever he wishes from them, and from the fruits [which grow] in Wadi Habib if they pile up on top of each other [because they fall and no one is tending the date palms and collecting the dates] and no one lives there, then there is no harm in him taking whatever he wishes from it."

Sahnun was asked about fruits of trees belonging to Muslims which lie between them and the enemy and from which the enemy have expelled them, so that they remain uninhabited: when Muslims are on a raid may anyone eat their fruits? He said, "If a numerous body of men are on a raid, then no, because it becomes valuable for that reason. If its owners had wished to sell it to the army they would have got a price for it. As for a small raiding party and the like, there is no harm that one passing by should eat from it, as opposed to a great body of fighters."

Dire Necessity

Malik said, "Someone who does not have anything and who asks his people to give him hospitality but they refuse, then let him eat what has not been slaughtered according to the shari'ah (al-maitah, which includes whatever has died of natural causes) unless he finds hanging dates which involve no cutting. As for that which is laid out on the ground to dry, if he is sure that he will not be considered a thief then let him eat, but otherwise let him eat what has not been slaughtered according to the shari'ah."

Alighting with a Dhimmi

Whoever alights with a *dhimmi* (one of the People of the Book living under Islam according to the contract of the *dhimmah* included in which is an obligation to extend three days hospitality to Muslims) must not take anything from him without his being contented with that. Someone asked, "What about the hospitality [for Muslims] which was imposed upon them?" He said, "It had been lightened at that time."

Masruq said, "Whoever is compelled by dire necessity to [eat] an animal which has not been slaughtered according to the shari'ah or has died of natural causes and he doesn't eat and so dies, will enter the Fire." Rabi'ah, Ibn Shihab and Malik said, "Wine is not permitted to a person in dire necessity. As for an animal which has not been slaughtered according to the shari'ah or has died of natural causes let him eat until he is satisfied, and then take some away as his provision for later until he finds something else to suffice him." Ibn al-Qasim said, "Even if the entire world were haram could one avoid living in it?"

Being cautious of haram wealth

Malik said, "When the sheep from the *sadaqah* (*zakat*) came, Ibn Hurmuz would not eat meat."

Malik said, "I disapprove of the food of someone who squeezes [grapes to make wine]." Bukayr used to accept gifts from a black woman in Egypt who sold an intoxicating drink. He said, "Because I used to see her spinning." (She earned money from the spinning as well as from the wine and so her income was not entirely haram). Al-Layth said, "If he has no wealth other than the wine then one should abstain from [accepting anything from him]."

The food and property of administrators

Al-Layth said, "I disapprove of the food of administrators ('*ummal* – means governors and people in administrative posts) from the perspective of scrupulousness without considering it haram." Abu Muhammad said, "He meant, and Allah knows best, those [administrators] who do not clearly forcibly expropriate [other's wealth]".[11] Al-Layth said, "There is nothing which is more serious, after [spilling] blood, than taking the property of people without right. Haram wealth enters into many things, from some of which the one who earns it cannot free himself: he marries a woman, a child is born to him and he has slaves and workshops."

Malik disapproved of the food of administrators who newly come into wealth, which previously they didn't have, because of their jobs.

Malik said, "Everyone who does some work for the Muslims has his provision from the Bait al-Mal. There is no harm in a gift with which a man is rewarded when the Imam (Khalifah or Amir) sees him worthy of that gift because of knowledge [he has] or because of a debt he owes, etc."

Malik said, "It has reached me that 'Umar made stipends of five thousand dirhams for some of the people of Badr."

Haram and halal wealth

Among what the people of Madinah say is that if someone uses haram wealth to buy a house or a robe without forcing anyone to buy that item, then there is no harm in your buying that house or that robe from the person who bought it with haram money. Ibn 'Abdus said, "That is when the [first] seller knows the defect in the sum of money paid." It is mentioned that Muhammad ibn Sahnun permitted it even if the seller didn't know the defect in the money paid. Ibn 'Abdus said, "If the purchaser gives you that house or that robe it is not permitted to accept it as a gift, since one whose wealth is encompassed by a debt is not permitted to give gifts or sadaqah."

Malik said about someone who had both haram and halal wealth, that if the haram that he had was a little amount among a great deal of halal then there is no harm in transacting with him. But if the haram is a great deal then one ought not to transact with him.

Usury

He said, "One should not transact with any Muslim who works with usury." He disapproved of exchanging a dinar for a Christian who had received it for selling wine or transacting with usury.[12] There is no harm in taking it from him in payment of a debt which he had before, just as Allah, mighty is He and majestic, permits taking the *jizyah* from them [even though much of their wealth is earned contrary to the shari'ah]. People other than Malik think that is less serious in the case of a Christian, since if he were to become a Muslim that which he owned would become halal for him.

Malik said, "There is no harm in your renting your house to a Christian or a Jew if he does not sell wine or pigs in it." Others say the same.

Malik said, "There is no harm in a Christian changing [coins] for you."

Chapter 10

Greeting

THE MESSENGER said ﷺ "Someone who is mounted should greet people on foot. When one of a group of people proffers a greeting, it suffices for all of them." He ordered ﷺ the widespread use of the greeting of peace.[1] Ibn 'Abbas said, "The greeting ends with 'barakah'," (i.e. *as-salamu 'alaikum wa rahmatullahi wa barakatuhu*). Ibn 'Umar used to say "*as-salamu 'alaikum*" whether greeting or returning a greeting.

Someone asked Malik, "Should one greet women?" He said, "As for older women, I do not disapprove of it. As for young women, I do not like it."

The Messenger 🕌 said about returning the greeting of Jews, "Say, '*Alaika* – upon you'[2]." Someone asked Malik, "Should someone who greets a Jew try to cancel or withdraw it?" He said, "No." Someone asked Malik, "Should they be addressed by honorific names?" Malik said, "I do not like them to be honoured, and they ought to be humbled." Others allow that as a dispensation because of the words of the Prophet 🕌 to a Jew, "Alight, Abu Wahb." Muhammad ibn 'Abd al-Hakam said that.

He said, "One ought not to say in greeting, '*salamu'llahi 'alaika* – the peace of Allah be upon you,' but rather, '*alaika's-salam* – upon you be peace,' or '*as-salamu 'alaikum*.'"

Kissing

Someone said to Malik, "What do you think about someone who comes home from a journey and his daughter meets him, or his sister, and kisses him?" He said, "There is no harm in that." He also said, "There is no harm in kissing one's daughter's cheek."

Someone asked, "Do you think that if his mother-in-law is an older woman she may kiss or embrace him?" and he disapproved of that.

Shaking hands and embracing

Malik was asked about shaking hands and he said, "People do that. As for me, I don't do it." He disapproved of a man embracing another man. He said, "Allah, glorious is He, said, '*Their greeting in it is "Peace"*,' (Surah Yunus, 10)." Other things have been narrated from him about shaking hands, i.e. that he shook the hand of Sufyan ibn 'Uyaynah and said to him, "If it were not for the fact that it is an innovation I would have embraced you." Sufyan used as an argument the Prophet's ﷺ embracing Ja'far when he returned from Ethiopia. Malik said, "That was especially for Ja'far," but Sufyan saw it as a general rule. In Malik's letter to Harun ar-Rashid, he permitted him to embrace his relative returning from a journey. Some say that it is not firmly established that this letter is Malik's.

It is related that the Messenger ﷺ said, "Shake hands with each other, it will drive away malice. Give gifts to each other and you will love each other and it will drive away rancour."[3]

Brotherhood for the sake of Allah

It is narrated that the Messenger ﷺ said, "If two become brothers for the sake of Allah, the most beloved of them to Allah is the one who most loves his companion."

'Umar said, "There are three things which will make your brother's love for you pure: that you should greet him before he greets you, that you should call him by the name he likes best and that you should make space for him in any gathering. It is sufficient as a defect in a man that he should bear a grudge towards people for something that appears to them from him when he is unaware of the same fault in himself, and that he should say things about someone in public which are no concern of his."

Shunning one's brother

Malik said, "The Prophet ﷺ said, 'It is not permitted for a Muslim to shun his brother for more than three nights, the two of them meeting and this one turning away and this one turning away. The best of them is the one who initiates the greeting'."[4] Malik said, "When he greets him he has discontinued shunning him."[5] He said in another place, "If he has harmed him, he becomes free of rancour [by greeting him]." Ibn al-Qasim said, "If he has not harmed him then greeting him is not an end of his shunning him if he continues to avoid talking with him. As for innovators, one is commanded to shun them." Sahnun added, "In order to discipline them."

Honouring others

Malik said, "Some say that a part of exalting Allah, exalted is He, is honouring an old man who is a Muslim[6]."

Someone asked, "Should a man stand for another who knows fiqh and who has a high standing and seat him in his place in a gathering?" He said, "That is disapproved of, but there is no harm in his making room for him."

Someone asked, "What about a woman treating her husband with exaggerated consideration, receiving him and taking off his garment and sandals and standing until he sits?" He said, "As for receiving him and removing [his garment and sandals] there is no harm in that. As for standing until he sits, no. This is one of the acts of tyrants. Often people wait for the tyrant, and when

he arrives they stand up. This is not one of the actions of Islam."
Some say, "That was done for 'Umar ibn 'Abd al-'Aziz when
he was first appointed at the time he went out to people and he
disapproved of it strongly, and said, 'If you stand we will stand,
and if you sit, we will sit. People only stand for the Lord of the
Worlds'[7]." It has been narrated that the Prophet ﷺ said, "Whoever
loves that people should present themselves to him standing, let
him prepare for his seat in the Fire."[8]

Malik was asked about a man who kissed the hand or the
head of a governor, or a freed slave who does that for his master.
He said, "That is not one of people's practices, but rather it is a
practice of non-Arabs." Someone asked, "What if he kisses his
father's head?" He said, "I hope that will be a light matter." In
another narration he was asked, "Should a man kiss his father's
or his uncle's hands?" He said, "I do not think he should. One
consideration is that those in the past did not do that."

Someone said, "When Ibn 'Umar returned from a journey he
used to kiss Salim, and he would say, 'A shaykh kissing a shaykh'."
He [Malik] strongly disapproved of the hadith and said, "We must
not narrate hadiths like these. Do not be destroyed by them!"

Seeking permission to enter

Malik said, "Permission [to enter a room or a house] is sought
three times. I do not like it being done more than that – that is
how it is narrated in the hadith – unless one knows that someone
hasn't heard, in which case there is no harm in doing it more times,

in order to be sure." He said, "It is an interpretation of the words of Allah, exalted is He, '*Until you seek permission*' (Surat an-Nur, 27-28) in that which is thought about it, and Allah knows best."

There is more on this topic in the chapter on covering the private parts.

Honouring older people

He was asked about someone who begins with older people and then proceeds to whoever is younger than himself, even though he [the older person] might not be better than him [the younger person]. He said, "There is no harm in it. Haven't you thought about when he makes space for him when he sits down, or works and earns something and then gives it to him." Someone said, "The people of Iraq say, 'Do not start with anyone before yourself even if it is your father'," and he disapproved of that. He said, "The Prophet ﷺ said to someone who wanted to speak before his companion, 'The older one, the older one!' He said to Abu Bakr when he brought his father to him, 'Why did you not leave the shaykh in his house?'"

Someone asked, "What about a man who writes a letter to another man, 'Convey my greetings to so-and-so-and-so-and-so'?" He said, "I hope that he is permitted and that he may have an excuse for that."

Asking for a blessing on someone who sneezes

Malik said, "Do not ask for a blessing on someone who sneezes until you hear him praising Allah. If he is far away from you and you hear those close to him asking for a blessing for him, then ask for a blessing for him." Whoever sneezes in the prayer should only praise Allah within himself. Sahnun said, "Not even within himself." The Messenger ﷺ said, "If he sneezes then ask for a blessing for him, then if he sneezes [again] then ask for a blessing for him, then if he sneezes say to him, 'You have a head cold'." In the book called, *The Abrogating and Abrogated* by Abu 'Ubayd he said that if one of a group ask for a blessing on him it suffices for the whole group as is the case in returning greetings. Yahya ibn Mazin said, "It is different from the case of returning greetings concerning the reply of one of the group [being sufficient]."

Returning to one's place in a gathering

Someone asked, "What about someone who stands up and leaves his seat, does he have more right to that place when he returns?" He said, "I did not hear anything from Malik about it. It is good [if he is allowed to sit in the same place as before] if he returns quickly, but if he returns later he cannot expect that. This is of the good qualities of character."

Private conversations and discussions

He was asked about four people, "Should three of them hold a discussion which excludes the fourth?" He said, "It is forbidden for them to leave one person out, even if they are ten people, in order to avoid bad opinion, envy and lying." However, some say that if it is with his permission there is no harm in it.

Honouring parents

A man who had a mother, a sister and a wife asked Malik, "Whenever she (his mother) sees me with anything, she says, 'Give this to your sister,' and she does this repeatedly. If I refuse her she curses me and supplicates against me." Malik said, "I do not think that you should anger her. Free yourself from her with whatever you are able, and hide what you have from her." He said, "Where shall I hide it? I have it in the house with me." He said, "As for me, I don't think that you should anger her and that you should free yourself from the displeasure of the two of them with whatever you are able."

Some say of Malik that a man said to him, "My father is in *bilad as-sudan*[9]. He wrote to me that I should come to him but my mother is preventing me from going." Malik said, "Obey your father and do not disobey your mother," and he disliked to tell him to disobey his mother. It is mentioned that al-Layth said that he should obey his mother since she has a right to two-thirds of filial respect. A man said to Mujahid, "My father calls me just as the prayer is beginning?" He said, "Obey him." Someone said to al-Hasan, "What is filial good treatment of parents?" He said, "That you give that which you possess to them liberally, and obey them when they command you as long as it doesn't involve disobedience [towards Allah and His Messenger]." Ibn al-Musayyab was asked about His words, mighty is He and majestic, "*And speak to them with nobility and generosity,*"[10] he said, "The words of a wrongdoing slave to his harsh master." Abu Hurayrah said, "Do not walk ahead of your father, and do not sit before him. Do not address him by his name and do not cause him to be cursed [by cursing another man's father thus making him retaliate by cursing your father]." Some say, "As for in the dark, then walk in front of him." Malik said, "Whoever does not reach his parents' old age or the old age of one of them, there is no harm if he says, '*My Lord, show mercy to the two of them as they did in bringing me up when I was small.*'"[11]

Chapter 11

The Fitrah, trimming the moustache, shaving pubic hair, circumcision, tooth-sticks, kohl, dyeing hair and tying it up, henna, cupping and entering public baths

The Fitrah – the natural condition of the human being

MALIK SAID, "The Messenger ﷺ said, 'Five things are of the fitrah: clipping the nails, trimming the moustache, plucking [the hair of] the armpits, shaving pubic hair, and circumcision'." Someone other than Malik said, "It has been narrated from Ibn 'Abbas concerning His words, glorious is He, '*When his Lord tried Ibrahim with some words,*'[1] that he said, 'It is the fitrah, and it is five things related to the head and five related to the body. In the head they are rinsing [out the mouth], sniffing [water up into the nose to clean it out], the toothstick, trimming the moustache and parting the hair. In the body they are circumcision, shaving the pubic hair, plucking [the hair of] the armpits, trimming the nails and cleaning the private parts with water after using the toilet."

The Messenger said ﷺ "If it were not that I should cause hardship to my Ummah I would have commanded them to use the toothstick."[2] And in another hadith, "You must use the toothstick."[3]

Malik was asked about someone who shaved off his moustache completely (*ihfa*) and he said, "He should be beaten painfully. This is an innovation. The *ihfa* which is mentioned in the hadith means trimming the moustache, and it means [trimming] the ends of the hair. 'Umar used to twist his moustache when something distressed him, and if it had been removed entirely he would not have found anything to twist."

Days for Massage and Cupping

He said, "I see no harm in massaging with oils, or cupping, on Saturdays, Wednesdays or any other days, and similarly travelling and getting married. I think it is a very serious matter that there should be a particular day on which one avoids that," and he rejected hadiths which have been narrated concerning these things.

Stopping work on Jumu'ah

Some of his companions disapproved of giving up work on the day of Jumu'ah in the same way as Jews treat Saturday with gravity or Christians treat Sunday.

Cupping

He was asked about cupping on the 17th, 15th and the 23rd [of the lunar month] and he disapproved of there being a particular day for that. It has been mentioned that al-Layth said, "I take care not to have cupping or massage with oils on Saturdays and Wednesdays because of a hadith which has reached me."

Malik said, "I have been told that the Messenger of Allah ﷺ said, 'If a remedy should reach illness, then cupping would reach it."[4] Someone asked Malik, "Should the locus of cupping on the back of the neck and in the middle of the head be shaved?" He said, "I disapprove of that, but I do not regard it as haram. What prevents him from washing [the hair] with marshmallow[5] and then cupping?" He said, "There is no harm if someone in need of a ghusl because of intercourse or ejaculation should have a massage with oils." Ibn al-Musayyab said, "There is no harm in being massaged with oils in the evening."

The time for clipping the nails, etc.

Malik said, "There is no particular period of time after the lapse of which one should repeat the clipping of nails, trimming the moustache and shaving pubic hair. It should be done when some time has elapsed." Someone asked, "What about the hair on one's head: is there some measure which when it reaches it, it should be parted?" He said, "I know no limit concerning that."

The beard and hair

He was asked about the length of the beard, when it becomes very long, and he disapproved of it. Someone asked, "Do you think that something should be taken off it?" He said, "Yes." Someone asked, "What about plucking out grey hairs?" He said, "I don't know it to be haram, but I prefer it to be left alone." Someone asked, "What about boys' locks of hair hanging down at the back?"

He said, "It is disapproved that some parts of the head should be shaved and other parts left alone." He asked, "What about cutting the hair and leaving a lock of hair hanging down?" He said, "I am not pleased at shaving the back of the neck nor cutting its hair for boys nor for girls."

He was asked about a woman braiding some of her hair as a bracelet and sending it to the people in the ribat[6]. He disapproved of that. I prefer that hair should be covered if it is shaved, and I think that discarding it is not very serious. He disapproved of hair being discarded at the (*Jamrah*) pillar (which the people performing Hajj stone) on the Day of Sacrifice (when men on Hajj shave their heads), or that any use should be made of that of it which is discarded or that it should be sold.

On another occasion he was asked about burying hair and nails. He said, "I do not think it should be done. It is an innovation. Some of the hair of the Messenger of Allah ﷺ was in the cap of Khalid ibn al-Walid. Some people disapprove of discarding blood on the surface of the earth, and they discard it in washing rooms or toilets (i.e. they go to great lengths to dispose of it), and this is an innovation. There is no harm in discarding blood on the ground."

Dyeing hair and hands

He was asked about dyeing [hair] black and he said, "I have not heard anything about it, and I prefer other dyes, and dyeing with henna and with *katam*[7] are permitted." Malik said, "The proof that the Messenger of Allah ﷺ did not dye [his hair] is that 'Aishah said, 'Abu Bakr as-Siddiq used to dye [his hair]!' for if the Prophet ﷺ had dyed [his hair] she would have begun with him."

Malik said, "The first community didn't have public baths. 'Umar ibn al-Khattab, 'Ali ibn Abi Talib, Ubayy ibn Ka'b and Ibn al-Musayyab didn't use to alter their grey hair. I saw Ibn Shihab dyeing with henna. There is no harm if a woman decorates her hand with henna or if she tints her hands' extremities without a dye." Someone said to him, "It has been said that she should either dye the hand entirely or leave it alone and that there is a hadith narrated about that from 'Umar," and he rejected that.

He said, "A woman ought not to tie up her hair with hair or anything else." Al-Layth said, "There is no harm if she ties it up with wool; it is only disapproved if done with hair." Someone asked Malik, "Should a woman place her gathered hair on top of her head?" He said, "There is no good in it." Someone asked, "What about a piece of cloth which she places on the back of her neck and ties up as a head scarf?" Malik said, "There is none of their contrivances which are less serious than these pieces of cloth, and I hope that there is no harm in it."

Malik spoke about a woman performing the Hajj who entered Makkah and whose head had become lice-infested so that it was bothering her. He was asked, "Do you think that she is permitted to shave it off?" He said, "I hope that it would not be very serious [if she does]. She has room to do that because of this overriding necessity. Many women come to ask for a ruling on that."

Kohl[8]

Malik said, "I disapprove of kohl at day or night for a man unless he has a reason. I never found anyone applying kohl like that except because of some imperative need." It has been narrated concerning kohl that one applies it an odd number of times. In the narration of Ibn Nafi' there is, "Should one apply Antinomy as kohl?" He said, "It is not one of the practices of the people [of Madinah] but I have not heard any prohibition of it."

Ibn al-Qasim was asked about going to public baths, and he said, "If you find them empty, or you go into them with other people who cover themselves, then there is no harm. If they do not cover themselves (i.e. their private parts) I do not think that you should enter them, even if you cover yourselves." Ibn Wahb used to go to the public baths along with everyone else. Then later he gave that up, and would only go alone. Someone asked, "Is there any measure for the size of the lower waist wrapper with which one should enter the public baths?" He said, "No." He said, "I disapprove of a woman entering the public bath even if she is ill, unless there is no one else with her."

Circumcision

Malik said, "I am not pleased with the circumcision of a seven day old boy. It is one of the practices of the Jews. There is no particular age at which it should be done. I prefer it to be done when they lose their first teeth. There is no harm if it is done before that or delayed until afterwards. I prefer any time after the loss of the first teeth."

He disapproved of calling the adhan in the ear of a newly born baby boy.

Malik said, "Women are the ones who should circumcise girls."[9] Others say, "It has been narrated that the Prophet ﷺ said, 'Circumcision is a Sunnah for men and a praiseworthy matter for women'." With respect to women it is known as *khifad* (lessening). The limits ought not to be exceeded when performing circumcision on women. It is narrated that the Prophet ﷺ said to Umm 'Atiyyah, who used to circumcise [girls], "Umm 'Atiyyah, cut off a little and do not injure [by complete surgical removal], because it is more wholesome for the face and its blood, and more likely to find good favour with the husband", meaning that it will be better for her health and it is better for her [husband when he has] intercourse [with her]." Malik said, "I prefer that women clip the nails, shave pubic hair and are circumcised just as men should." He said, "Whoever buys a female slave may have her circumcised if he wishes to keep her. If she is for resale then that is not his responsibility."

CHAPTER 12

COVERING THE PRIVATE PARTS, WHAT COVERING IS REQUIRED
OF WOMEN AND MEN, MIXING OF THE SEXES IN EATING
TOGETHER AND AT THE TIME OF SLEEP, GOING ALONE WITH
CLOSE RELATIVES AND OTHERS, AND A WOMAN'S TRAVELLING
WITH SOMEONE OTHER THAN A CLOSE RELATIVE

The Hijab

THE PROPHET ﷺ referred to "Women who are clothed [yet] naked". 'Aishah said, "May Allah have mercy on the Ansari women; when the ayah concerning the veil[1] was revealed they resorted to the thickest of their garments[2] and put them on their heads."

Malik said, "Women used to go out in the time of the Prophet ﷺ. 'Umar said, 'Your women ought not to go out like that,' and then the ayah concerning the veil was revealed. Apartments used to be made of palm branches, and their sides were covered with coarse hair cloths so that the interiors could not be seen."

Seeking permission to enter

Someone asked Malik, "Do you consider that *'Those you own as slaves should ask your permission...'* (Surat an-Nur, 56)[3], applies to people today?" He said, "I hope that it was only before doors and screens were made use of, and that it no longer applies to people, since when anyone goes alone he closes the door and lowers a curtain." Someone asked, "Do you think that the *qubbah* (a tent-like structure on the back of camels in which women sit) is sufficient?" He said, "Yes."

Performing sexual intercourse naked

Someone asked, "May a man make love to his wife without any screen between him and her?" He said, "Yes." Someone said, "They narrate that it is disapproved." He said, "Consider what they narrate as null and void. The Prophet 🕮 and 'Aishah 🕮 used to perform *ghusl* together naked, and it is even more appropriate to be naked in intercourse." He said, "There is no harm in looking at the private parts in intercourse."

Someone asked, "May one enter a public bath with a lower garment while some of those within it do not have lower garments?" He said, "It doesn't please me."

Servants and slaves

Someone asked, "May the wife's female servant see her husband's thigh?" He said, "No. Allah, glorious is He and exalted, says, '*And those you own as slaves*'.[4] Nor should his wife's servant enter while he is in the bathroom, nor his son's servant or his father's servant. There is no harm in him uncovering his thigh in front of his family."

Someone asked, "May his eunuch[5] servant see his thigh uncovered."
He said, "That is not so serious."

He said, "There is no harm in a man's waistwrapper coming underneath the navel and revealing the navel if he has a large stomach."

He strongly rejected the behaviour of Madinan slave-girls in
going out uncovered above the lower garment. He said, "I have
spoken to the Sultan about it, and have received no reply." He
said, "Beat slave-girls if they do that." He said, "There is no harm
in it if she wraps her clothes around her." Someone asked, "Can
a woman throw off her outer wrapper in front of a eunuch whom
she or someone else owns, and he is one of those who do not have
sexual desire[6]." He said, "There is no harm in it unless he is free, in
which case, no." In another narration he said, "If he is a slave and
if he is of low intelligence." He said, "The entrance of her husband's
eunuchs upon her, old or young, is clearly less serious than others'
eunuchs." He said, "There is no harm in a woman who has a slave
boy of low intelligence and poor appearance, if he sees her hair, her
shoulders and her feet. As for a good-looking boy, he may not." As
for her husband's slave boy of low intelligence, he disapproved of
that. One of the men of knowledge used to allow a water-carrier
to come in among his family. Someone asked, "What about a boy,
half of whom is free and half of whom she owns, may he see her
hair?" He said, "I do not like it."

Women family members

He said, "If someone goes in to see his mother or his sister I prefer him to ask permission before he goes in."

He said, in the *Muwatta'*, "Someone asked, 'May a woman eat with someone other than a relative whom she would be unable to marry or with her slave-boy'." He said, "There is no harm in that if it is in manner which is recognised as normal behaviour for a woman to eat with others." 'Ali ibn al-Jahm said, "He meant an old woman past childbearing age. She may eat with her husband and others, but she should not be alone with someone to whom she is not related in such a way as to be unable to marry him."

There is no harm in a man seeing his mother-in-law's hair, but she ought not to embrace him when he returns from a journey, even if she is past the age of childbearing. As for his sister-in-law let him keep his distance from her as much as he is able. I think that someone should go before women when they sit with craftsmen. A young woman should not be left alone sitting with craftsmen. As for older women and servants and those upon whom no suspicion could fall because of their sitting with him, and if he is also one upon whom suspicion could not fall, then there is no harm. There is no harm if a woman should take off her outer garment in the presence of her son-in-law.

He said, "Aishah ⬥ veiled herself in the presence of a blind man. Someone said, 'He can't see you.' She said, 'But I can see him'."

Someone asked, "Should we look at the hair of Christian women who are the wet-nurses of our children if we cannot avoid it?" He said, "It doesn't please me."

Ibn Wahb said, "Malik said, 'There is no harm if a woman washes in the open without an outer garment. Ibn Jurayj informed me from 'Ata that the Prophet ﷺ saw a man in al-Abwa[7] bathing naked from a pond in a field, and he said, "Truly Allah is modest and He loves modesty, and He veils[8] and loves concealment. So if any of you bathes let him cover himself"[9].'"

Someone asked Malik, "Should servants spend the night naked under one sheet," and he rejected that strongly. Someone asked, "May one allow one's son to sleep in a bed with another six year old boy without any cloth between them?" He said, "I prefer that some cloth is placed between them."

Women travelling

Malik said, "It is disapproved for a woman to travel for a day and a night without a male relative whom she would be unable to marry. There is no harm if a woman performs Hajj in a group of women and men who are trustworthy, among whom there is no male relative whom she would be unable to marry."

There is more on this matter in the chapter on travel.

He said, "The boy child with whom she was suckled is her brother and he is a male relative whom she is unable to marry." Someone asked, "What about her husband's son [from another marriage]?" He said, "Allah, mighty is He and majestic, says, '*Your mothers are forbidden to you [in marriage]...*' and the rest of the ayah

(Surat an-Nisa', 23. See notes for the complete ayah).[10]" He said, "This refers to the degrees of male relatives who may not marry a woman. As for a man wishing to travel with a woman, whom his father had divorced, and who had subsequently remarried a number of times, I don't like that." Someone asked, "What about a woman who cannot find someone of an equivalent social standing except for a man who is not one whom she would be unable to marry?" He said, "No," and he forbade it.

Someone asked, "On a journey, could one carry a slave woman by whom one's father has had a child?" He said, "If he draws her close to himself, then it does not please me."

Someone who went on Hajj said that there was a woman with them who needed someone to carry her and there was no male relative whom she could not marry who could be close to her. "My view was that he should stoop enough that she could place her foot on his back, and that was because of the pressing need of the situation." He meant that if any way had been found around that he wouldn't have done it.

Ibn Wahb said, "There is no harm in a man kissing a six-year old girl and the like of her."

Malik said about a man who had sexual intercourse with his slave girl, "There is no harm if he sends her to the market to acquire his necessities. The free woman may go out for her necessities. Asma' used to lead her husband az-Zubayr's horse on the road when she was pregnant."

Chapter 13

Food and drink, washing the hands, and eating with the left hand, drinking standing, and other things on food and drink and responding to invitations, hospitality, the hospitality of the people of the dhimmah. Also skinning an animal that has died of natural causes and using its bones

Eating and drinking

THE PROPHET ﷺ forbade a man eating with his left hand or drinking using his left hand. In one hadith there is that the Messenger of Allah ﷺ ate fresh dates with watermelon, one in one hand and one in the other.[1] When he ﷺ drank he used to give the drink to person on his right.

He said ﷺ "Name Allah [by saying *"Bismillah* – in the name of Allah"] and eat from that which is closest to you."[2]

He ﷺ forbade blowing into drinks, and he forbade drinking from silver vessels.

It is narrated that he ﷺ drank while standing. Malik said, "Umar, 'Uthman and 'Ali used to drink while standing and in my view there is no harm in it."

He said ⁕ "The Muslim eats in one gut and the kafir eats in seven guts."[3] This is a metaphor for eating a great deal or a little. It has also been said that it is about one particular man. Someone said, "Rather, the disbeliever who eats little, if he becomes a Muslim, would eat even less because of the blessing of pronouncing the name of Allah over his food."

He ⁕ would not eat garlic, leeks or onions because he used to speak to Jibril, upon him blessings and peace. He forbade whoever eats any of these from coming to the mosque, so that he does not cause offence to people by his breath.

Malik said, "Blowing on either food and drink is disapproved."

Someone asked, "May one eat and place his hand on the ground." He said, "I beware of doing that myself, but I haven't heard anything about it." Someone else said, "It has been narrated that the Prophet ⁕ said, 'As for me, I do not eat reclining'."[4]

Someone asked Malik, "May a man eat food which neither his family and dependants nor his companions eat, and dress in something other than that in which he clothes them?" He said, "Yes, by Allah! I think that he is permitted to do that, but he should treat them well." Someone asked, "What about Abu Dharr's hadith?" He said, "People at that time didn't have this food [that we have today]."

Someone asked, "Should one who eats with his wives and children eat from what is in front of them?" He said, "There is no harm in it."

Someone asked, "What about ravenous people who are eating, and each of them eats from in front of each other and they allow each other to do something like that?" He said, "There is no good in the like of that. It is not one of the qualities of character which are recognised among us. The Messenger ﷺ forbade eating two dates together," and in one hadith, "unless his companions allow it."[5] Malik said, "There is no good in coupling dates, i.e. eating two or three dates in one mouthful." He said in another narration, "Because they share in it." Ibn Nafi‘ narrated from him that, "If he is the one who fed them then it is alright," but in the narration of Ibn Wahb he said, "That is not good." Others say, "A similar situation pertains to figs."

When the Prophet ﷺ used to eat dates his hand would go around the dish.

Malik said, "There is no harm in drinking from the mouth of the water-skin, and no prohibition of that has reached me." Someone said, "What about from the broken edge of the drinking vessel or what is near to the handle?" He said, "I have heard some things, but I have not learnt anything about it," and it was as if he regarded [what he had heard] as weak.

Someone asked, "May one clean one's hands with flour?" He said, "Something other than it is preferable to me, but if one does it, I don't think there is any harm in it. 'Umar ﷺ used the inner part of his foot as a napkin."

Ibn Wahb narrated that there is no harm in cleansing oneself with chickling vetch or grass peas, beans and the like of that, and in rubbing oneself with them in the public bath. He used to oil his body in the public bath to protect against cracking of the skin. In the narration of Ashhab, "He was asked about cleansing oneself (*wudu'*) with flour, bran and beans and he said, 'I have no knowledge about it. Why would one purify oneself with it? If something incapacitates one, one should purify oneself with dust'."

Self-indulgence

He said, "Umar said, 'Beware of this self-indulgence, and the customs of the non-Arabs,' and I disapprove of washing hands before food[6], and think that it is one of the customs of the non-Arabs."

Wedding feasts and invitations

He, upon him blessings and peace, commanded us to accept invitations [to wedding celebrations].[7] Someone said to Malik, "If someone is invited to a wedding, should he accept it if there is drink at it?" He said, "One should abandon it, because it is making something objectionable very public." Someone asked, "What if there is entertainment and trumpets?" He said, "If there is a great deal of it and it is conspicuous, I disapprove of it." Rabi'ah said, "Accepting invitations is only recommended to establish the marriage and witness it, because open displays [of misconduct] are destructive." Malik granted licence to stay away from weddings in which there is overcrowding.

Someone asked Malik, "What about a Christian who prepares a feast and invites me, should I accept it?" He said, "I do not like it, but I don't know it to be haram." Someone said, "Umar stayed away from one."

He was asked about invitations to circumcisions and feasts, and he said, "These are not the invitations [referred to in the hadith], so if one accepts them there is no harm. However one is only obliged to accept invitations to wedding feasts."

He was asked about that which they scatter on the children at the time of the emergence of a child's teeth, which the children snatch up. He said, "I do not like that if they snatch."

Hospitality

Malik spoke about the hadith of the Prophet ﷺ concerning hospitality, "Its kindness is for a day and a night," and he said, "One shows hospitality to the guest in an excellent manner and is generous to him and honours him, gives him gifts, and one singles out a day and a night for that. Hospitality is for three days and anything after the three days is an act of sadaqah."

Malik said, "A traveller who alights with a dhimmi may not take anything from him but that which he voluntarily gives." Someone said, "What about the hospitality of three days which was imposed on them?" He said, "That was at that time, but then it was lessened for them."

Making use of dead animals which have not been slaughtered correctly

Malik said, "Some say about the skin of an animal which has not been slaughtered according to the shari'ah, 'Every skin which has been tanned is pure,' but I myself beware of it ." He said, "There is no harm in dressing in fox furs if they have been slaughtered correctly." He said, "There is no harm in using bones from an animal which has been slaughtered. There is no good in those which are from an animal which has not been slaughtered correctly, combs made from them should not be used to comb the hair, and one should not oil oneself in them." He was asked about the bones of an animal which had not been slaughtered, whether one may make molten silver run through their ashes? He said, "No, and no benefit may be derived from any part of the animal which has not been slaughtered."

Chapter 14

CLOTHING, SILK, MATERIALS WOVEN OF MIXES OF WOOL AND
SILK, DYED MATERIALS, DRESSING IN WOOL, LETTING THE
LOWER GARMENT HANG DOWN AND WRAPPING ONESELF IN ONLY
A SINGLE PIECE OF CLOTH, SEAL-RINGS, JEWELLERY, GOLD AND
SILVER VESSELS, WEARING SANDALS, IMAGES AND SCULPTURES,
AND MENTION OF THE FORM OF THE PEOPLE OF THE DHIMMAH

Clothing

THE PROPHET ﷺ said about white clothing, "Dress in white and shroud your dead in it, because it is some of your best clothing."[1] He said about gold and silk, "These two are haram for the males of my Ummah and halal for its females."

He said ﷺ "On the Day of Resurrection, Allah will not look at one who drags his lower garment[2] from exultant pride," and in another hadith, "his robe from vain and self-conceited pride."[3] He said ﷺ "The lower garment of the believer reaches to the middle of his lower leg. There is no wrong to be counted against him respecting what is between that and the ankles. What is below that is in the Fire."[4] He forbade ﷺ *ishtimal as-samma'*.[5]

Malik said, "Voluminous clothing is disapproved, and I disapprove of lengthy clothing."

Suf – wool

Someone asked, "What about wearing rough wool?"[6] He said, "There is no good in fame and notoriety due to one's clothing. If he were to wear it one time and remove it another I would hope [that it would be acceptable], but as for persistently [wearing wool] so that one becomes known and famous for it, I do not like it. There is some coarse cotton which is a similar price but less likely to attract attention. The Prophet ﷺ said to that man, 'Let your wealth be seen upon you'. 'Umar used to dress in fine new garments. He used to say, 'I prefer to see the Qur'an reciter dressed in white clothing'."[7] Malik said in another instance, "I do not disapprove of someone who has nothing else wearing wool, but I disapprove of someone who has something else wearing it. I prefer that he should conceal his deeds, and that was what the people who preceded us used to do." Someone asked, "What if he only means to show humility in his dress?" He said, "You can find cotton for the same price as wool."

Revealing clothing

Someone asked, "May a man wear a thin shirt?" He said, "If the lower garment is thick then there is no harm if the shirt is fine, if it is moderately priced and not an extravagance. I disapprove of servant- or slave-girls dressing in the *Qaba* (a tunic with a split to the rear) because it exposes their posteriors."

He was asked about *as-Samma'* and he said, "It is when one wraps a cloth around the shoulders and then brings one's left hand out from underneath the garment having no lower garment on. There is no harm in it if one has on a lower garment." He later said about it, "It does not please me," (i.e. perhaps even if there is a lower garment.)

Caps (*qalanis*)

He was asked about caps[8] and he said, "They used to be worn of old in the time of the Prophet ﷺ and before that. Khalid ibn al-Walid had a cap in which there was a hair of the Prophet ﷺ and it was the one which he wore when he fought on the day of al-Yarmuk[9]."

Umbrellas and the Hawdaj

Someone asked, "What about umbrellas?" He said, "They were not a part of people's attire but I see no harm in them."

Some say that the first to make use of the large Hawdaj[10] carriers [on the backs of camels] was al-Hajjaj.

Covering the head with a robe

Malik was asked about covering one's head with one's robe and he said, "If it is because of heat or cold or for some other reasonable excuse, there is no harm in it, but if it is for any other reason, then no. Abu'n-Nadr always did it because of the heat." He said, "Sakinah, or Fatimah, the daughter of al-Husayn saw one of her sons covering his head and she said, 'Uncover your head, because covering the head is a cause of uncertainty at

night and it puts one in a low and despicable condition by day'.'"
Malik said, "I disapprove of it if there is no reasonable excuse,
but I do not know that it is forbidden. It is not the attire of the
best people."

'Umar forbade women dressing in thin white linen clothes and
he said, "Even if it is not transparent it does describe." Malik said,
"He meant that it clings to the body." There is more material of
this nature in the chapter on covering the private parts.

Turbans and sandals

Malik said, "Turbans, crouching with the belly against the back
of the legs [sometimes with a garment wrapped around the legs
and the back to prevent one from falling], and wearing sandals are
practices of the Arabs, and they do not exist among the non-Arabs.
The turban was used in the beginning of Islam and it continued to
be used until these people appeared. I have not found anyone of any
standing who did not wear the turban, Yahya ibn Sa'id, Rabi'ah and
Ibn Hurmuz. I used to see thirty-one men wearing the turban in
Rabi'ah's circle and I was one of them. Rabi'ah would not take it off
until the Pleiades had risen. He used to say, 'I find that the turban
increases the intellect'." Someone asked, "Should one let some of
it hang down between the shoulder-blades?" He said, "I never saw
any of those I came upon letting some of it hang down between the
shoulder-blades, but they would let it hang in front of them. I do not
disapprove of letting it hang down behind because it is forbidden,
but because this is more beautiful, and because those I met used to

do it except for 'Amir ibn 'Abdullah [ibn az-Zubayr ibn al-'Awwam] who used to let it hang down between his shoulder-blades, and he said, 'Jibril 🕮 was seen in the form of Dihyah al-Kalbi and he had let some of his turban hang down between his shoulder-blades'. I disapprove of wearing a turban without putting some of it under the chin (a custom still observed in Morocco and Algeria until today). However, whoever does that in his own house when he washes or when he is ill, then there is no harm in it."

Malik was asked about sandals and he said, "I prefer them rounded and shortened, with a heel and a back part." He said, "I saw the sandals of the Prophet 🕮 and the dimensions which they had, which was shortened, their shortening from the back, heeled at the rear. Each sandal had two thongs."[11] Malik said, "There is no harm in donning sandals while one is standing. One should not walk wearing only one sandal unless one is one-legged.

Rings

"I disapprove of wearing a seal-ring on the right hand." He said, "One eats, drinks and works only with one's right, so how would one want to take hold of something with one's left hand and then work?" Someone asked, "Then should one turn the seal in towards the palm?" He said, "No." Someone asked, "May one use the seal on the right hand for some need which one remembers, or tie a thread on a finger?" He said, "There is no harm in that." It is narrated that the Prophet 🕮 used to wear a silver Ethiopian ring, and it is narrated that he used to wear a ring with Carnelian. It is narrated that the inscription on his ring was, "Muhammad is the Messenger of Allah" and some say that it was, "There is no god but Allah, Muhammad is the Messenger of Allah," and he used to seal his letters with it. The Khulafa and Qadis have their names engraved on their rings. Some say that the inscription on Malik's ring was "Allah is enough for me and excellent as a guardian."[12] Malik said, "There is no good in inscribing an image on the seal of a ring." Someone asked, "If there is mention of Allah on it and one wears it on the left hand, may one use it to wash one's private parts after the toilet?" He said, "I hope that it is not a very serious matter."

Gold and silver

Someone said to Malik, "May one tighten the waist-belt, which is one of the customs of non-Arabs, over clothing when one intends to travel?" He said, "I hope that there is no harm in that. I disapprove of putting a pin of gold into the seal of the ring or mixing it with a grain or two of gold so that it does not tarnish."[13] He said, "There is no harm in strengthening teeth with gold." Someone asked, "Has it reached you that one of the Companions lost his nose and so he had a nose made from gold?" He said, "No." He disapproved of women wearing iron bracelets. He said, "It has reached me that 'Aishah disapproved of it, and that whenever she saw iron anklets on a child's leg she used to order their removal."

Malik said, "I do not like oiling oneself, washing one's private parts, eating or drinking from a silver vessel or from a drinking vessel covered with silver or in which is a circle of silver, and similarly mirrors in which there is a circle of silver. I disapprove of gold eardrops for small boys." In another narration there is that he disapproved of gold for boys. Someone asked, "Do you hope that it might be something that is not too serious?" He said, "I hope so. I disapprove of children wearing silk."

Silk

Malik said, "Silk should not be worn in military expeditions nor at any other time. I don't know of anyone who is taken as an exemplar who wore it in military expeditions." Someone asked, "What about wearing a material woven from wool and silk?" He said, "I don't know it to be forbidden, but I am happier with something else. Wearing clothes made from a cloth whose warp is silk doesn't please me, nor cloth striped with silk." Someone asked, "What about night-garments on which there are silk markings to the measure of about two fingers?" He said, "I do not like it, but I do not think that it is forbidden." In another narration he said, "There is no harm in fine thread." (Perhaps meaning that some silk thread doesn't matter). Ibn Bukayr narrated from Malik that there is no harm in a man donning an ihram in which there is the measure of a finger of silk."

Someone asked, "What about a mount with a saddle-covering of bright red?" He said, "I don't know it to be forbidden."

He said, "Ata ibn Yasar used to dress in upper and lower garments coloured with saffron and I saw Ibn Hurmuz and

Muhammad ibn al-Munkadir doing it, and I saw a perfume oil on his head.[14] I saw 'Amir ibn 'Abdullah, Rabi'ah and Hisham ibn 'Urwah parting their hair and they did have hair." Rabi'ah said, "I saw some shaykhs in Madinah who had locks of hair which fell down, wearing clothes dyed with red with a touch of yellow and rose-coloured shirts, and they had staffs in their hands and traces of henna, in the way that young men in the prime of life do. The *deen* of any one of them was more remote than the Pleiades if anyone wanted to say what his *deen* was like."

Sculpted forms and images

Malik said, "If figures and forms which are on brass vessels, jugs, couches and domes are sculpted so as to give them a three dimensional form it is more serious. It has reached me that the first sculpted form used was upon the death of a prophet whom they sculpted so that they could console themselves with the form. It continued like that until it was worshipped." He said, "Abu Talhah al-Ansari removed a floor-covering from underneath him because of the images that were on it because of what the Messenger of Allah ﷺ had said about images. Sahl ibn Hanif said to him, 'Do you not say "except for whatever is a marking on a piece of cloth"?' He said, 'Certainly, but I feel happier about it'."[15] Abu Salamah said, "There is no harm in (the presence of images on) everything which is walked upon or worn." Malik said, "I prefer leaving it. Whoever leaves that for which there is licence without declaring it to be forbidden there is no harm for him in it."

I disapprove of a man buying images for his daughter or placing images on the bezel of his ring.

The People of the Dhimmah

Malik said, "I think that Christians should be compelled to wear belts, and that used to be required of them of old. I think that they should be compelled to be humble. 'Umar wrote that they should be mounted sideways on donkeys."

CHAPTER 15

MEDICINE, CAUTERISATION, TREATMENT, CHARMS, SEEKING
PROTECTION, AMULETS, AUGURY, THE [EVIL] 'EYE', THE
PLAGUE, TREATMENT FOR [POSSESSION BY] JINN, AND THE
STARS (ASTROLOGY)

Medicine and doctors

THE MESSENGER of Allah ﷺ said to two men who were treating a wounded man, "Which of you is more skilful in medicine?" He said, "He sent down the remedy Who sent down illnesses."[1]

Sa'd ibn Zurarah was cauterised because of an ulcerous condition of the throat, and 'Abdullah ibn 'Umar was cauterised because of facial paralysis and he was charmed against a scorpion.

It is narrated that 'Umar prevented a sick man from eating what worsened his illness. He said, "Umar prevented me from eating so much that I used to suck on a date-stone from hunger."

The Prophet ﷺ ordered the use of charms to protect against 'the eye' and the performance of wudu' for it.

Malik said, "I think that the Imam should prevent doctors from treating people, except for well-known and recognised ones. Rabi'ah said to me, 'Do not drink any of their remedies except for something which you know: I enjoin that upon you'."

He was asked about a pregnant woman for whom a drink is prescribed and he said, "As for that of which you have no fear then there is no harm in it. As for that which is feared then no."

Ibn Wahb said, "Yahya ibn Sa'id disapproved of drinking something to prevent pregnancy." Rabi'ah said, "Whoever dresses his wife with a gem[2] or a bead in order for her to become pregnant or in order for her not to become pregnant then this is one of the views which is hated."

Someone asked Malik, "May a wound[3] be washed with urine or wine?" He said, "If he washes it out with water after that, then yes. I deplore the use of wine in remedies and other things. It has reached me that the only one who puts these things in remedies is someone who wants to challenge the *deen*. Urine is less serious in my view."[4] Ibn al-Qasim narrated that he disapproved of the use of wine in treatments even if it is later washed with water. He said, "It has reached me that Ibn 'Umar's slave told him that he had treated his camel with it and he disapproved of it."

Malik said, "Human urine may not be drunk for medicinal purposes, but there is no harm in drinking the urine of the eight types of grazing livestock which Allah, glorious is He, has mentioned[5]." Someone asked him, "Every one whose meat may be eaten?" He said, "I only said the urine of grazing livestock. There is no good in the urine of female donkeys." Someone asked him, "What about the ewe which urinates in the vessel while it is being milked?" He said, "There is no harm in it."

Talismans, amulets, charms and supplications of refuge and protection

Someone asked, "May the Qur'an be written [as a talisman] for someone who has a fever?" He said, "There is no harm in it nor in using any good words as a charm. There is no harm in hanging a talisman for protection in which there is Qur'an and mention of Allah if it is protected in leather." Someone said, "They make knots[6] in the string with which they attach it." He said, "There is no good in it." Someone asked, "May one put the seal of Sulayman[7] in the talisman of protection?" He said, "There is no good in it."

Someone asked, "May someone who makes the charm do so while she has iron in her hand?" He said, "I disapprove of that." Someone said, "Then with salt?" He said, "It is less serious." In another narration he said, "May we charm with iron and salt?" and he disapproved of all of that. Tying knots in string is more strenuously disapproved.

The Prophet ﷺ told us to exercise charms against 'the eye'. 'Aishah said, "When the Prophet ﷺ had a complaint he used to recite over himself the two surahs of seeking refuge (*al-Mu'awwidhatan* – surahs 113-114, Surat al-Falaq and Surat an-Nas) and then blow [lightly with a little spittle][8]. When his pain became very severe, I used to recite over him and wipe [him] with his hand hoping for its blessing."[9] He said to 'Uthman ibn Abi'l-'As when he had a pain, "Wipe it with your right hand and say:

$$\text{أَعُوذُ بِعِزَّةِ اللهِ وَقُدْرَتِهِ مِنْ شَرِّ مَا أَجِدُ}$$

'I seek refuge with the might of Allah and His power from the evil of what I experience'."[10]

There is something narrated from the Messenger of Allah ﷺ concerning a man who found it difficult to urinate:

$$\text{رَبُّنَا اللهُ الَّذِي فِي السَّمَاءِ نُقَدِّسُ اسْمَكَ، أَمْرُكَ فِي السَّمَاءِ}$$
$$\text{وَالْأَرْضِ، كَمَا رَحْمَتُكَ فِي السَّمَاءِ فَاجْعَلْ رَحْمَتَكَ فِي}$$
$$\text{الْأَرْضِ، وَاعْفُ عَنَّا حَوْبَنَا وَخَطَايَانَا، أَنْتَ رَبُّ الْعَالَمِينَ}$$
$$\text{فَأَنْزِلْ شِفَاءً مِنْ شِفَائِكَ وَرَحْمَةً مِنْ رَحْمَتِكَ عَلَى هَذَا الْوَجَعِ}$$

"Our Lord Allah who is in the heaven, we declare Your name free of every imperfection. Your command is in the heaven and the earth. Just as Your mercy is in the heaven put Your mercy on earth. Obliterate our pain and our wrong actions. You are the Lord of the creatures, so send down some of Your healing and some of Your mercy upon this pain."

Someone asked Malik, "May a gem be suspended [as an amulet or talisman] because of erysipelas[11] (St. Anthony's fire)?" He said, "I would hope that this is not so serious."

Someone asked, "What about something suspended under the ceiling on which an iron tool is put?" He said, "I would hope that this is not so serious."[12]

He was asked about amulets and charms to cure possession by jinn using trees and oils? He said, "There is no harm in that. It has reached me that 'Aishah suffered from insomnia, and someone said to her in a dream, 'Take the water from three wells each of which flows into the other and bathe yourself with it.' She did it and that which she had experienced left her."

Ibn Wahb said, "I do not disapprove of the people of the Book doing charms [for medicinal purposes upon the Muslims]. I base myself on the hadith about Abu Bakr when he said [to the Jewish woman charming 'Aishah who was sick], 'Charm her with the Book of Allah'[13]. I do not base myself on Malik's disapproval of it."

Al-Layth said, "There is no harm in hanging some Qur'an [as a talisman] on a woman confined in labour and on sick people if some leather protects it, or if it is in a piece of tubing but I disapprove of iron tubing. I saw in one hadith that one should write for the pregnant woman whose delivery is difficult for her:

$$\text{حَنَّى وَلَدَتْ مَرْيَمَ، مَرْيَمُ وَلَدَتْ عِيسَى، اُخْرُجْ يَا وَلَدُ،}$$
$$\text{الْأَرْضُ تَدْعُوكَ اُخْرُجْ يَا وَلَدُ}$$

'Hanna gave birth to Maryam; Maryam gave birth to 'Isa. Come out, child! The earth calls you: come out child!' The one who narrated the hadith said, 'Often a ewe would be in labour and I would say it, and I would not have left it before it gave birth."

Cauterisation

Malik said, "There is no harm in cauterisation. Ibn 'Umar used cauterisation because of facial paralysis and Sa'd ibn Zurarah because of an ulcer in the throat."

Omens and augury

The Prophet ﷺ used to disapprove of evil augury but he was pleased with good omens. He disapproved of bad names. He said, "There is no contagious disease, no evil omen, no night-bird of ill omen[14], and no Safar.[15]" The best of them is the good omen and 'the eye' is true. He said ﷺ "Ill luck is in a horse, a woman and a dwelling." In another hadith, "If there is ill luck then it exists in three things," and he mentioned these three.[16] He said to the man concerning the house in which his family had left and all his wealth had gone, "Leave it as blameworthy."[17]

The [Evil] 'Eye'

It is narrated that the Prophet ﷺ said, "If anything were to outstrip, then 'the eye' would outstrip it."[18] He said ﷺ to 'Amir when he looked at Sahl ibn Hanif so that he became unwell [and passed out], "For what reason does any of you kill his brother? Did you not ask for a blessing for him? 'The eye' is true. Perform wudu' for him." In another narration it is "wash for him", so 'Amir washed his [own] face for him and his hands, elbows, knees, feet, and the inner part of his waistwrapper in a vessel and then poured the water on him. Sahl recovered consciousness among the people without any harm.

Malik said about 'the inner part of his waistwrapper' that is that which is under the waistwrapper which is close to the body. Ibn Nafi' said, "The inner end of the waistwrapper which hangs down." Ibn Habib said, "That which the person donning the waistwrapper first puts on upon the right side of his waist."

Ibn Habib said, "Az-Zuhri said, 'The one who has 'the eye' is brought a vessel in which is water. He puts his two palms in it and then washes out his mouth. He wipes his hands in the vessel, washes his face in the vessel, then he puts his left hand in and uses it to pour water over his right hand, then pours with his right hand over his left hand. Then he pours with his left hand on his right elbow, then with his right hand on his left elbow, then with his left hand on his right foot then with his right hand on his left foot, then with his left hand on his right knee and then with his right hand on his left knee, all of that being done in the vessel. Then he washes the inner part of his waistwrapper in the vessel. He does not place the vessel on the ground, and pours it on the head of the one affected by 'the eye' from behind him with one pour which flows over his body'."

The jinn and possession

Malik was asked about someone who had a slight mental derangement or possession by jinn to whom someone else said, "If you wish to kill your companion [the jinn], we will kill him." Malik said, "I have no knowledge of this. This is a part of medicine."

He said, "There was a mine from which people were continually receiving misfortunes from the jinn. They complained of that to

Zayd ibn Aslam and he told them to call the adhan, each man calling the adhan and raising his voice with it. They did that and it stopped."

Astrology

Malik was asked about someone who reflects on the stars and says, "The sun will be eclipsed tomorrow, and so-and-so will come," and the like of it. He said, "I think that he should be prevented and if he gives up [well and good], but if not he should be taught a serious lesson. The one who treats the knowledge of the unseen is a liar. If anyone had known that the Prophets would have known that. A poison[19] was put in a sheep for the Prophet ﷺ and he knew nothing about it until it spoke."

Gazing on the leprous

Malik was asked, "Do you disapprove of gazing incessantly on the leprous?" He said, "As for fiqh, I have not heard anything about its being disapproved. I think that the prohibition that has been narrated concerning that is only lest it causes fear, because of something that occurs in oneself."

The Plague

The Prophet ﷺ said about the plague, "If you hear of it in a land then do not advance towards it. If it occurs in a land when you are there, do not flee from it."[20] Malik was asked whether going to a land in which death and illnesses occur is disapproved and he said, "I see no harm whether one goes or remains where one is." Someone said, "Is this like that which has been narrated in the hadith of the plague?" He said, "Yes."

Chapter 16

UsING DOGS, HANGING TALISMANS AND BELLS ON ANIMALS,
BRANDING ANIMALS, CASTRATING ANIMALS, STUDS, SNAKES
AND ANTS, ETC.

Dogs

THE MESSENGER ﷺ forbade using dogs except for animal husbandry and agriculture, and he commanded ﷺ that dogs be killed.

Someone asked Malik, "Is it alright to kill dogs?"[1] He said, "Yes, those of them which cause harm should be killed, and those (harmful dogs) which are in a place they shouldn't be, such as a gathering place for people." Someone said, "The people in agricultural regions make use of dogs in their houses because of the riding animals which are in them." He said, "I don't think that is right. The hadith only refers to animal husbandry and agriculture – and I don't think that it resembles the guard-dog – and those camels, cows, sheep and goats which are in the deserts. As for those which are in the houses, they don't please me." Someone said, "What about if one is afraid of thieves opening the doors and driving away the riding animals?" He said, "It does not please me." Ibn al-Qasim said, "Only if it pastures with the animals and then returns with them."

Someone asked Malik, "What about a traveller who takes a dog along for protection?" He said, "It does not please me." Someone asked, "What about traders in animals who put their animals out to pasture and who make use of dogs?" He said, "They are livestock."[2]

Someone asked, "What about a city-dweller who uses a dog for hunting?" He said, "That is only allowed for someone who uses it to gain a livelihood not for sport." He said, "There is no harm in using dogs for any kind of livestock, but it must be without purchase. I disapprove of its being purchased." Ibn Kinanah and others said, "There is no harm in buying a dog since it is permitted to make use of them."

Bells around the necks of camels and donkeys

Someone asked Malik, "May one hang bells on the necks of camels and donkeys?" and he disapproved of it. Someone asked, "What about necklaces?" He said, "I have not heard of any disapproval of that except in the case of the necklace made of sinew."

Branding

He said, "There is no harm in branding livestock as long as it is not in the face because that is disapproved. There is no harm in doing it on the ear of the sheep since the wool of its body would conceal the brand. As for camels and cattle they are branded elsewhere since their furs and hair are not like those of sheep and goats." He was asked, "What do you think about some people who have a very old brand and another man wants to make use of one which is similar?" He said, "He may not do that, because he will make things doubtful for them when they seek their stray animals and camels which have died."

Spurs

He was asked about spurs for riding animals which might cause them to bleed? He said, "I hope that it might not be so serious."

Castration

Malik said, "Umar used to disapprove of castration and say, 'In it is the completion of the creation'." Malik said, "There is no harm in castrating livestock if it is good for the meat. I disapprove of gelding horses, and I have heard that it is disapproved. There is no harm in gelding others such as mules and donkeys, etc." Malik said, "If a horse is angry and obstinately refuses [to obey] there is no harm in gelding it."[3]

He said, "There is no harm in allowing a donkey to mount an Arabian mare. When what is in the wombs of mares and of stud-mares has difficulty in coming out, there is no harm in a man putting his hand into its vulva to help it." Someone asked, "If the stallion is ill-natured may another male be allowed to mount him in order to break him?" He said, "I don't know that it is forbidden, but it is not a good way of doing things." He said, "I disapprove of small boys riding horses which are being raced for wagers. There is no harm in beads and gems being hung on horses if they are for decoration."

Snakes

Malik was asked whether snakes which inhabit houses and which suddenly appear should be warned for three [days before being killed]? He said, "The hadith[4] refers to Madinah, and I think that it is also a good mode of conduct elsewhere." He said that snakes found in the desert should be killed and that they should not be approached in the houses.

Lice, flies and ants

He said, "I disapprove of killing lice and midges with fire, for this is an exemplary punishment. I disapprove of killing flies and small ants in the Haram or while in ihram." Someone asked, "What about a person who is not in ihram killing many small ants or ordinary ants because they are harming him?" He said, "It doesn't please me." He was asked about ants which damage a roof and he said, "If you are able to refrain from harming them then do so, but if they cause you harm and you are not able to leave them alone, then I hope it is permissible to kill them."

Gecko lizards and frogs

It is narrated that the Prophet ﷺ ordered that gecko lizards should be killed[5] and it is related that he prohibited the killing of frogs.[6]

CHAPTER 17

TREATING SLAVES AND ANIMALS WELL, WOMEN, PROTECTING
ONE'S NEIGHBOURS, ORPHANS, ANTICIPATING A REWARD FROM
ALLAH FOR DISASTERS, MENTION OF DAUGHTERS, AND MENTION
OF THE MEANING OF THE WORD *BID'*

Slaves[1]

IT IS related that the Prophet ﷺ said, "I advise you [to treat] the two weak ones [well]: women and slaves."[2] He said ﷺ "A slave has a right to his food and clothing in kindness. He must only have work imposed on him which he is able to do."[3]

Someone asked Malik, "Did 'Umar use to go out to the groves of date-palms to lighten the burden on those slaves who had been charged with work which was too heavy, and to increase the slave's provision from the little of his own provision?" He said, "Yes, and for those free men who were labouring with work they could not manage." Someone said, "The governors order that loads should be lightened for whoever passes with a heavily-burdened camel or mule." He said, "They have done correctly, but their innovation of coercing slaves to work on the frame-posts [for the pulley-system at the head of a well] is disapproved."

Someone asked, "Can someone who has a slave who harvests in the daytime employ him in milling at night?" He said, "As for that work in a well-recognised manner which does not exhaust them, there is no harm in it. If there is exhaustion from the work done in the day he should not be employed in milling at night."

Someone asked, "What about a slave who complains of his being unmarried and asks his master to sell him saying, 'I have found a situation'?" He said, "He doesn't have to do that. If this were the case, [all the] servants would say it. Masters do not have to sell their slaves except if they are suffering harm from them." Someone asked, "What about a slave whom a man wants to buy and he asks him, for the sake of Allah, not to buy him?" He said, "I prefer that he leave him, but as for my giving a decision against him, I won't!"

Sayyid and Rabb

Someone asked, "Does anyone in Madinah disapprove of him saying to his master, 'O my master – *Ya Sayyidi*'?" He said, "No. Allah, glorious is He, says, '*And the two of them found her master at the door*'[4] and He says, mighty is He and majestic, '*A master and one who is chaste*'."[5] Someone said, "They say, 'The *Sayyid* is [only] Allah'." He said, "Where do they find that in the Book of Allah? There is only '*Rabbana, Rabbana* – Our Lord, our Lord!' in the Qur'an, and *Rabbi*, '*My Lord, forgive me and my parents*'. (Surah Nuh, 28). " Someone asked, "Is supplicating saying, '*Ya Sayyidi* – O my Master' disapproved?" He said, "I prefer that one should supplicate with what is in the Book of Allah and with the supplications of the Prophets."[6]

Spurring camels on the Hajj

He said, "There is no harm in moving quickly on the Hajj on one's mount, but I disapprove of spurs, and they do not work, and if he does a lot of it he will tear a hole in it. The Prophet ﷺ passed by a donkey which had been burned on the face and he found fault with that." Malik was asked after that, and someone said to him, "May he goad it to the extent of causing it to bleed?" He said, "There is no harm in that."

Feeding and clothing dependants

Someone asked, "May one eat food which one's dependants and slaves do not eat, and dress in clothes the like of which one does not clothe them in?" He said, "I think that one is permitted to do that, but one must dress them and feed them with kindness." Someone asked, "What about the hadith of Abu'd-Darda'?" He said, "They didn't have this food in those days." Malik said, "I disapprove of a man being asked about the food which he brings into his house."

Women

Malik said, "One ought not to try to surpass a woman in unbecoming language, nor dispute with her a great deal nor try to get her to turn back." 'Umar ibn al-Khattab said, "There are none who are deficient in intellect and *deen* who more overpower men of intelligence in their affairs than women." It is narrated that woman is created from a crooked rib, and that if you straighten her you will break her – and breaking her is divorcing her – and that if you leave her as she is you will enjoy [being with] her, crooked as she is.[7] It is narrated that Ibrahim ﷺ complained of Sarah to Allah, mighty is He and majestic, and Allah revealed to him, "Live with her according to how she is as long as there is no corruption in her *deen*." Malik said, "A man asked the Messenger ﷺ 'Should I lie to my wife?' He said, 'There is no good in lying.' He said, 'May I promise her and say things to her?' He said, 'There will be no crime written against you'."[8]

Neighbours

It is narrated that the Prophet ﷺ said, "Whoever believes in Allah and the Last Day then let him honour his neighbour generously,"[9] and that he said ﷺ "Jibril counselled me about neighbours so much that I thought he would make them inherit."[10]

Orphans

He said, "I and the one who takes care of his or someone else's orphan, if he has fear of Allah, will be in the Garden like these two".[11] It is narrated in a hadith that Allah, glorious is He, will purify a house in which there is an orphan who is honoured generously.[12] He said, "Be like a compassionate father to orphans." A part of the reward for orphans is that they should be disciplined moderately with kindness for their own benefit.

Afflictions and anticipating a reward from Allah

He said ﷺ "Nothing afflicts a believer, even a thorn which pricks him or stone which bruises his foot or severe repression of his anger when someone is enraged at him, but that Allah, exalted is He, will expiate some of his wrong actions by it."[13] In one hadith there is, "Whoever is afflicted with some disaster and anticipates [a reward for it from Allah] will have blessings and mercy from Allah," and this is as Allah, glorious is He, says, *"The ones who, when an affliction happens to them, they say"*... up to His words, *"Those they are the guided."* (Surat al-Baqarah, 155-6)[14]

It is narrated that the Prophet ﷺ said, "Whoever is tried by anything from his daughters and keeps company with them in a good manner, then they will be a screen for him from the Fire."[15]

He said ﷺ "If three children of any of you Muslims die and he anticipates [that Allah will recompense him for them] they will be a shield for him from the Fire." Someone said to him, "Messenger of Allah, or two?" He said, "And two."[16] In another hadith it is, "[If] three children [of any of you Muslims die] and the Fire touches him it is only to fulfil the oath."[17]

The meanings of Ashudd and Bid' (some)

Malik said, *"Al-Ashudd* (Surah Yusuf, 22)[18] is puberty," and some say also that it is thirty years old. He said, "It has reached me that the word *bid'* (Surah Rum, 2) means a number between three and nine. Yusuf ﷺ was cast into prison when he was a boy." Others narrate that he was nineteen years old. Allah, glorious is He says, *"And We revealed to him, 'You will tell them of this affair of their's at a time when they are unaware'."* (Surah Yusuf, 15)

CHAPTER 18

TRAVELLING, WOMEN TRAVELLING, VOYAGING BY SEA, AND
COMMERCIAL JOURNEYS TO ENEMY LANDS

Travelling

THE MESSENGER ﷺ said, "Travelling is a piece of torment which prevents any of you from his sleep, his food and his drink. So when you attain your object from the point of view of your journey hasten to your family."[1]

The du'a of travelling

When he ﷺ placed his foot in the stirrup he used to say:

بِسْمِ اللهِ، اللَّهُمَّ أَنْتَ الصَّاحِبُ فِي السَّفَرِ وَالْخَلِيفَةُ فِي الْأَهْلِ،
اللَّهُمَّ أَزْوِ لَنَا الْأَرْضَ وَهَوِّنْ عَلَيْنَا السَّفَرَ، اللَّهُمَّ إِنِّي أَعُوذُ بِكَ
مِنْ وَعْثَاءِ السَّفَرِ، وَكَآبَةِ الْمُنْقَلَبِ، وَسُوءِ الْمُنْظَرِ فِي الْأَهْلِ
وَالْمَالِ

"In the name of Allah. O Allah You are the Companion on the journey and the Khalifah in the family. O Allah contract the earth

145

for us and make the journey easy for us. O Allah I seek refuge with You from the difficulty of travel, and from the grief of the place where one returns, and from finding [that] something evil has happened to one's family and wealth."

Travelling in company

He said ﷺ "One is a shaytan, two are two shaytans, and three are a mounted party."[2] He said ﷺ "Shaytan busies himself with one and two, and when they are three he does not busy himself with them," meaning on travel. He said ﷺ "You should travel at night because the earth is contracted then as it is not contracted in the daytime."[3]

Women travelling

He said ﷺ "It is not permitted for a woman who believes in Allah and the Last Day to travel for a day and a night except in the company of a male relative whom she could not marry."[4]

Travelling with the Qur'an

He ﷺ forbade us travelling with the Qur'an to enemy lands for fear that the enemy might gain it.

Travelling for trade

Malik was asked about travelling to enemy lands for trade and he said, "I think that they should be prevented from doing that." It has reached me from Sahnun that he said, "Whoever travels by sea in search of the world and goes to the land of the enemy then that is his wound[5]."

Women travelling to Hajj or 'Umrah

Someone asked Malik, "Can a woman travel to Makkah with someone who is not a guardian?" He said, "She may go with a company of people, trusted people with whom she has no fear for her person," meaning that the prohibition is only of her travelling for some other purpose than an obligatory duty with someone other than a *mahram* (male relative whom she would be unable to marry).

Malik said, "There is no harm in someone who comes back from a journey at night returning to his family at that hour."

Malik said, "No one had more right to what was in the saddlebags of 'Abd al-Wahhab ibn Bukht than his travelling companions."

Travelling by sea

Malik said, "Umar ibn al-Khattab asked 'Amr ibn al-'As about the sea and he said, "A strong creation upon which a weak creation rides, like maggots on a piece of wood. If they get lost they perish and if they survive they are separated.' 'Umar said, 'I will never convey anyone on it'. Then Mu'awiyah asked his permission to travel on it and he refused him permission. He asked 'Uthman after that and he refused. When he repeated the request he wrote to him, 'If you travel on it with your family and your children,' and so he travelled on it with his wife. 'Uthman was the first to convey anyone on it. Then later 'Umar ibn 'Abd al-'Aziz took the position of 'Umar ibn al-Khattab and did not convey anyone on it until he died."

CHAPTER 19

Genealogies

IT IS related that the Messenger ﷺ said, "Truly Allah has removed from you the pride of the age of ignorance and its boasting about its ancestors. [There is only] a believer who is fearful of Allah or a wicked person who will be grievous. You are the descendants of Adam and Adam was from dust."

A man who knew genealogies was mentioned to the Prophet ﷺ and he said, "A science which does not benefit and ignorance of which does no harm." It is mentioned that 'Umar said, "Learn as much of your genealogies as will allow you to keep connections with your relations."

Names

He said ﷺ "The best names are 'Abdullah and 'Abd ar-Rahman."[1] He ﷺ used to deplore bad names such as 'Harb – War', 'Murrah – Bitterness', 'Jamrah – Firebrand', and 'Handhalah – a very bitter fruit' and he ﷺ changed the names of more than a few of those who accepted Islam.

Malik said, "A man ought not to be named Yasin, nor Mahdi, nor Jibril." Someone asked, "What about al-Hadi – the Guide?" He said, "This is nearer, since al-Hadi is the one who guides on the path."

Malik said, "There is no harm in a boy receiving an honorific name before puberty."

He said, "The newborn child is only named on the seventh day."

He said, "There is no harm in a Christian who accepts Islam changing his name but he should not be attributed to anyone other than his father nor should he say, 'Ibn 'Abdillah or Abu 'Abd ar-Rahman'."

He said, "I do not know of any harm in being named 'Muhammad' along with the honorific ' Abu-l-Qasim'."

He said, "The people of Makkah narrate, 'There is no house in which there is [someone with] the name Muhammad except that they will experience good or be provided for'."

Extending genealogies back to Adam or Ibrahim

He said, "I disapprove of anyone extending his genealogy back until it reaches Adam or Ibrahim." He said, "Who informed him about those between him and Ibrahim? I disapprove of anybody extending back the genealogies of any of the Prophets – and the Prophets, the blessings of Allah be upon them, are not like others – saying, 'Ibrahim son of so-and-so, son of so-and-so.' Who told him this?"

Malik said, "A man's honorific name is often used as his name. The names of Abu Salamah and others were their honorific names."

Malik said, "Ali ibn al-Husayn [Zayn al-'Abidin], al-Qasim ibn Muhammad and Salim ibn 'Abdullah were the sons of slave women."

Interpreting dreams

Malik said, "The Prophet ﷺ said, 'Nothing remains of prophethood except for bringers of good tidings.' They said, 'What are bringers of good tidings, Messenger of Allah?' He said, 'A good dream which a right-acting man sees or which someone else sees for him is one of forty-six parts of prophethood'."[2]

He said ﷺ "The good dream is from Allah and the bad dream is from shaytan.[3] Whenever anyone of you sees something which he dislikes then let him spit lightly to his left three times when he wakes up and seek refuge with Allah from its evil, for it will not harm him if Allah wills."

Someone asked Malik, "May anyone interpret dreams?" He said, "Does he want to play with prophethood?" Malik said, "No one should interpret dreams except for someone who does it well. If he thinks that it is good he should tell him, and if he thinks it is bad then let him say something good or be silent." Someone asked, "Should he interpret it in a good way when he actually thinks that it is bad because of those who say, 'It will turn out according to how it is interpreted'?" He said, "No. Dreams are a matter of prophethood, so that one would be playing with one of the matters of prophethood. The Siddiq said ﷺ concerning the dream of 'Aishah[4] when the Messenger of Allah ﷺ died, 'This is one of your moons and it is the great one of them.' This was his interpretation and he disliked to speak at first [when she had the dream] and he said, 'Good.' If anyone had wished to transform [the outcome] by his interpretation to something other than its true nature, Abu Bakr would have desired to avert [the death of the Messenger] with an interpretation by which the Messenger of Allah ﷺ would have remained alive. He did not think that was permissible and so he said, 'Good, if Allah wills,' and was silent."

CHAPTER 20

POETRY, SINGING AND ENTERTAINMENT, BACKGAMMON AND
CHESS, AND RACING AND ARCHERY

Poetry

THE MESSENGER said ☙ "Some poetry is wisdom and some
rhetoric is magic." He said, "It would be better that the belly
of any of you should be full of pus than for it to be full of poetry."
[1]He said, "No one has composed a verse of poetry like the one
who said [in *tawil* verse form]:

"Everything without Allah is false,

And every pleasure – no avoiding it – perishes."[2]

He said, upon him blessings and peace, "I am not concerned
with play and entertainment."[3]

Malik was asked about reciting poetry and he said, "Go lightly
with it and do not do it a lot. One of its defects is that Allah, glorious
is He, says, '*We did not teach him poetry and it is not fitting for him*' (Surah
Yasin, 69)."

Singing

About His words, "*There are some people who trade in entertaining
tales...*" (Surah Luqman, 5) Mujahid said, "Singing." Al-Qasim
said, "Singing is a part of falsehood."

Drums and musical instruments

Malik was asked about beating the large tablah drum, and about a reed-pipe whose sound reaches one and which one experiences as pleasurable, in the street or in a gathering, and he said, "Let him stand up if he finds pleasure in that, unless he has sat down for some need that he has or is unable to stand. As for in the street, then let him turn back or move on ahead [but not linger]."

He said, "What about a prepared meal to which people are invited and at which there is entertainment?" He said, "It is not right for anyone possessing any honour to attend sport and play." Someone asked, "What about entertainment in which there is a trumpet?" He said, "If there is a great deal of it and it is well known, I do not approve of it."

He said, "There is no harm in a tambourine at a wedding." Asbagh said, "It means that instrument which is like a sieve and which is uncovered at one end." There is some licence to beat a large tablah drum at weddings.

In the chapter on accepting invitations there is more on this subject.

Al-Hasan [al-Basri] said, "If there is entertainment at a wedding they have no [right to expect that people should accept their] invitation."

Games

It is narrated that the Prophet ﷺ said, "Whoever plays backgammon then the anger of Allah and His Messenger is on him."[4] Malik disapproved of all games such as backgammon and 'fourteen'. He disapproved of chess about which he said, "It is more distracting [from the remembrance of Allah] and it is worse." Someone asked, "Should one greet people who play them?" He said, "Yes. They are the people of Islam." When someone does such a thing to excess he introduces an innovation. The testimony of one who does it constantly is not accepted.

Wagers and Prizes

It is narrated that the Prophet 🕮 said, "There is no wagering except on horses, mules and asses,[5] or camels,[6] or archery and spear throwing."[7]

Ibn al-Musayyab said, "There is no harm in [two riders] wagering upon [their] horses if there is a *muhallil*[8]." He said, "There is no harm in two men placing a wager, one man placing his wager and the other placing his wager, and with them there are people who do not place wagers. If one of them wins he takes the wagers and if he is beaten then there is nothing against him."

But Malik did not say this. What is permitted according to Malik is that someone outside the race, such as the Imam,[9] sets a prize which whoever wins takes. There is no harm if the one who sets the prize races his horse along with them. Then if he wins, the prize goes to the second in the race, if there are a number of horses. However if there are only two horses and the one who sets the prize wins, then the prize is used to feed whoever attends the race.

It is also narrated from him that there is no harm if the one who sets the prize stipulates that if he is beaten he [the other] takes that prize, but if he [himself] wins he preserves the prize (and the first will be his prize) whether he placed the prize externally, whether he won or someone else won.

It is similar in the case of archery and spear-throwing.

The term *musalli*[10] means the one who comes second behind the winner, and it is called that because its lip is at the *sala* of the winner, i.e. the root of the tail. The tenth is called *as-sukait* and those after the second up to the ninth have no special name except according to the number of their place in the race.

CHAPTER 21

THE HIJRAH, MILITARY EXPEDITIONS AND HISTORY

IN THIS chapter there is material which has been memorised from Malik but most of it is from other men knowledgeable about the battles and history.

Persecution

They say that the Messenger of Allah ﷺ remained patient for thirteen years under the afflictions caused by the idolaters, warning those who mocked him. The trial became so severe for his Companions that he permitted some of them to emigrate to Ethiopia.

Jihad

Then the first ayah which was revealed to the Prophet ﷺ concerning jihad was the words of Allah, glorious is He, *"Permission is granted to the ones who are being fought because they are wronged and truly Allah is able to help them..."*[1] and the subsequent ayats.

Then later *"Fight them until there is no persecution*[2] *and the deen is for the sake of Allah..."* (Surat al-Baqarah, 193) was revealed.

Hijrah

When Allah granted permission for war and the Ansar pledged allegiance to him at al-'Aqabah[3] the Messenger of Allah ordered his Companions to emigrate to Madinah, and so they went one after another. The Prophet ﷺ stayed after them waiting for Allah to grant him permission to emigrate. No one remained behind with him of the emigrants except for those who had been imprisoned or persecuted, and Abu Bakr and 'Ali. Whenever Abu Bakr asked permission of the Messenger of Allah, he said, "Do not be in a hurry; perhaps Allah will give you a companion." Abu Bakr hoped that it would be him. He bought two riding camels and got them ready for that. The Messenger of Allah ﷺ did not fail to come to the house of Abu Bakr at the two ends of the day.

The day Allah granted him permission to emigrate he came to Abu Bakr during the full heat at midday. When Abu Bakr saw him, he said to himself, "He has only come at this time because something has happened." When he came in, he gave up his seat for him and he sat down. He ﷺ told him that Allah had permitted him to emigrate. Abu Bakr said, "Companionship, Messenger of Allah?" and he said, "Companionship," and Abu Bakr wept for joy and told him that he had prepared two riding camels for that. He sent the two of them with 'Abdullah ibn Arqat[4] to pasture them.

No one knew of the emigration except Abu Bakr and 'Ali. Abu Bakr said, "He told 'Ali to stay behind to return those things which had been entrusted to him." Then he and Abu Bakr went out through a gap at the back of the house to a cave in Thawr, a mountain beneath Makkah, which they entered at night. Abu Bakr told his son, 'Abdullah, to find out what people were saying and then come to them in the evening with that information. He told 'Amir ibn Fuhairah, his freed slave, to pasture his flocks and then bring them to the cave in the evening.

Asma' bint Abi Bakr used to bring them food in the evening, and so they stayed in the cave for three days.

Quraysh set a prize of one hundred she-camels for him.

When three days later people had given up on them, the man they had hired brought them the two riding beasts. Asma' brought them travelling provisions but she forgot to bring a cover for them, so she gave them the *nitaq* (the garment which she wrapped around her waist) and so was named the Possessor of Two *Nitaq*s because she split it in half and wrapped the other half around her waist.

The Messenger of Allah ﷺ mounted the better of the two mounts, but he would not take it without paying its price. Abu Bakr made his freed slave, 'Amir ibn Fuhairah, ride behind him so that he could serve them on the journey. Their guide was 'Abdullah ibn Arqat. Malik said, "The name of their guide was Raqit and he was a kafir." Musa ibn 'Uqbah said, "His name was Urayqit."

Suraqah ibn Malik ibn Ju'shum followed them on his horse, because the idolaters had put a price of one hundred she-camels on his return. Suraqah said, "When the people came into view, my horse stumbled under me, its two forelegs sank into the ground and I fell off. It withdrew its foreleg and a smoke like a whirlwind came out with it, and so I knew at that point that he was being protected from me. I called the people saying, 'I am Suraqah, wait for me so that I can talk to you.' The Prophet ﷺ said to Abu Bakr, 'Ask him what he wants.' He asked me and I said, 'Write me something.' He told Abu Bakr to write something for me on a bone or on a rag and then he threw it to me. I met him carrying it on the Day of the Opening of Makkah at al-Ji'ranah."

Arrival in Madinah

Malik said, "History is dated from the Messenger of Allah's arrival in Madinah."

'Urwah ibn az-Zubayr said, "The Messenger of Allah ﷺ alighted in Quba' on the Monday of the new moon of Rabi' al-Awwal when the morning light was strong. Musa ibn 'Uqbah said, "Monday of the new moon of Rabi' al-Awwal." They said, "He stayed with Sa'd ibn Khaythamah in the stony tract of Bani 'Amr ibn 'Awf of the Ansar." Some also say that it was with Kulthum ibn al-Hadam. There is no disagreement that in Madinah he stayed with Abu Ayyub, whose name was Khalid ibn Zayd. He ﷺ resided with him until his residence and mosque were built.

They say, "He mounted and departed from Bani 'Amr [in Quba'] on the day of Jumu'ah and passed by Bani Sulaym among whom he prayed the Jumu'ah. Some say that he stayed for three nights with Bani 'Amr." Ibn Shihab and others say, "He stayed with Bani 'Amr from thirteen to nineteen days and then he rode on."

The mosque of Quba and the mosque of the Messenger of Allah

The mosque of Quba' was built. Some say that it is the one which is "*founded upon fear of Allah*"[5] but it is also said that it is the mosque of the Messenger of Allah ﷺ which is also narrated from the Prophet ﷺ and is more firmly established according to the men of knowledge. Malik and others say that. The site of the mosque was a yard in which dates were dried and which belonged to two orphans of the Ansar who were in the care of As'ad ibn Zurarah. He ﷺ bought it from them and then built it as a mosque.

Marriage to 'Aishah

In Shawwal of that year he first dwelt with 'Aishah, may Allah be pleased with her, at the beginning of eight months after the Hijrah.

'Ali married Fatimah, the pleasure of Allah be on both of them, but it is also said that it was in the second year at the beginning of twenty-two months [after the Hijrah].

The Second Year of the Hijrah

Malik said, "In it was the expedition of al-Abwa[6] which the Messenger of Allah ﷺ himself went on with only Muhajirun." Ibn 'Uqbah said, "The first expedition which the Prophet ﷺ went on took place in Safar at the beginning of twelve months after his arrival in Madinah. He reached al-Abwa and then returned and sent sixty men of the First Muhajirun and some say, eighty mounted men, along with 'Abdullah ibn al-Harith." Some also say that he sent Hamzah out with thirty mounted men, and that then later he raided in Safar.

'Abdullah ibn az-Zubayr was born and he was the first child born to the Muhajirun in Madinah.

The Change of the Qiblah

Some say that on Tuesday in the middle of Sha'ban, the Qiblah was changed during Salat adh-Dhuhr.

Ramadan

During Sha'ban, fasting the month of Ramadan was made obligatory.

Zakat al-Fitr

The Messenger of Allah ﷺ ordered Zakat al-Fitr.

Some say that on Monday three days before the end of Rabi' al-Akhir he went on an expedition until he reached Buwat intending [to fight] Quraysh, and that later he returned without meeting any opposition.

In Jumada al-Ula, he ﷺ went out to al-'Ushairah which is in between Makkah and Madinah.

In Jumada al-Akhirah, he went out until he reached a valley called Safwan[7] in search of Karz ibn Jabir al-Fihri who had raided the cattle of Madinah. He went out in search of him but did not find them.

In Rajab he sent Sa'd ibn Abi Waqqas with a group of eight men.

In Rajab he sent 'Abdullah ibn Jahsh to Nakhlat where he met the caravan and killed Ibn al-Hadrami on the last day of Rajab. It was about that the ayah was revealed, *"They ask you about the sacred month about killing in it..."*[8]

During Sha'ban the Prophet ﷺ went out in search of the milch camels until he reached Yanbu' when he returned with the milch camels and those with them.

Badr

He took war counsel on going to Badr, Badr the Greatest Assault (Surat ad-Dukhan, 15), to which he went on Wednesday evening after eight days of Ramadan. Malik said, "Among three hundred and thirteen men." Al-Awza'i said, "Three hundred and fifteen." Someone said, "...seventeen." There were eighty-one Muhajirun men among them. Some also say that there were ninety-three Muhajirun and their confederates, and that the rest were Ansar. Nobody came with them but men from Quraysh or their confederates or their freed slaves, or men from the Ansar, their confederates or their freed slaves. Some say that there were one hundred Muhajirun of whom eleven were freed slaves. They met the idolaters on the Jumu'ah morning. Malik said, "It was the seventeenth day of the month of Ramadan, one and a half years after his arrival in Madinah." The idolaters were between nine hundred and a thousand with one hundred cavalry. The Muslims only had two horses, but it has also been said that there were three: the horse upon which az-Zubayr sat, al-Miqdad's horse and the horse upon which Abu Murthad al-Ghinawi sat.

Malik said, "On that day the Messenger of Allah ﷺ asked how much the idolaters ate every day? Someone said, 'Ten or nine slaughtered camels a day.' He said ﷺ 'The people are between a thousand and nine hundred'." They say that he left Abu Lubabah in charge of Madinah and that Ibn Umm Maktum led the prayer. Some also say that he left 'Uthman ibn 'Affan in charge.

Malik said, "There were few *shuhada'* on the day of Badr. There were a similar number of prisoners to the number of idolaters who were killed: forty-four men." Someone else said, "Thirteen Muslim men were killed as *shuhada'* on the day of Badr, four from Quraysh and nine from the Ansar." It has been said, "Fourteen, eight from the Ansar and six from the Muhajirun." Fifty idolaters were killed, and some say seventy and there were a similar number of prisoners.

The Messenger of Allah ﷺ sent Zayd ibn Harithah and 'Abdullah ibn Rawahah with the good news of Badr to Madinah.

Ruqayyah the daughter of the Messenger of Allah ﷺ died. 'Uthman had remained behind from Badr because of her. A share of the spoils of the battle was apportioned to him.

He ﷺ returned from Badr on Wednesday, eight days before the end of Ramadan.

There was the expedition against Qarqarah al-Kudr. News of the assembled flocks of Sulaym and Ghatafan reached him ﷺ. So he went out in the first nights during the new moon of Shawwal and returned ten days later without meeting battle, driving flocks of sheep, goats and cattle.

Ten days into Shawwal there was the expedition of al-Mughnimah on which he sent Ghalib ibn 'Abdillah al-Laythi. They encountered the tribes of Sulaym and Ghatafan. They killed some and took some flocks, and returned sixteen days into Shawwal. Three Muslims were killed as *shuhada'*.

'Ali took up residence with Fatimah.

The raid of as-Saweeq. It reached the Prophet ﷺ that Abu Sufyan was advancing on Madinah and so he ﷺ went out to meet them nine days before the end of Dhu'l-Hijjah. Abu Sufyan and his companions fled flinging away their provisions, so their companions said to them, "You only went out drinking as-Saweeq."[10] Then he returned eight days before the end of Dhu'l-Hijjah without engaging in battle. Ibn 'Uqbah said, "This raid was in 3 AH in Sha'ban."

Some say that in this year al-Hasan ibn 'Ali was born.

The Third Year of the Hijrah

Some say that it was in mid-Ramadan of this year that al-Hasan ibn 'Ali was born. In it Fatimah conceived al-Husayn, because there was only one period of purity between him and al-Hasan, and some say that there were fifty nights [between them].

The Prophet ﷺ married Hafsah, the daughter of 'Umar, and Zaynab bint Khuzaimah. He married 'Uthman to his daughter Umm Kulthum.

The expedition against Bani Fatyun whom the Prophet ﷺ announced that he would make war upon or expel. They were expelled without fight to Syria.

At the end of Muharram there was the expedition against Dhu Amr which is also known as the raid of Bani Anmar[11] on which the Messenger of Allah ﷺ went himself. He succeeded in it and divided camels [between the warriors], returning after five days of Safar.

Bani Qaynuqa'

In Safar there was the expedition against Bani Qaynuqa' (a Jewish tribe). They besieged them and they surrendered.

Also the expedition against Buhran. He went out at the new moon of Rabi' al-Akhir intending Quraysh and Bani Sulaym until he reached Buhran, a mine in the Hijaz in the district of al-Furu'. He returned at the beginning of Jumada al-Akhirah without meeting battle.

Uhud

In it was the battle of Uhud to which he went on the evening of the Jumu'ah on the fourteenth of Shawwal. Malik said, "Both the battles of Uhud and Khaybar were at the beginning of the day." Someone else said, "Sixty-five Muslims, of whom four were Muhajirun, were killed as *shuhada*'." Malik said, "Four Muhajirun and seventy Ansar were killed." In the time of the Prophet ﷺ there was no battle which was more severe than it or in which more people were killed.

166

They say that the next day, on returning from Uhud after sixteen nights had passed of Shawwal, he went out to Hamra al-Asad. It is eight miles from Madinah. Abu Bakr and az-Zubayr were the first to respond to Allah and the Messenger on that day after they had been wounded.[12]

The raid of ar-Raji'.[13] Some say that there were six men at ar-Raji' one of whom was Khubayb ibn 'Adi.

The Fourth Year of the Hijrah

Bi'r Ma'unah

There was the group who were sent to Bi'r Ma'unah which is about four days' journey from Madinah. 'Amir ibn at-Tufayl, along with Bani Sulaym and [some of] Bani 'Amir, killed them. Some say that 'Amir ibn Fuhairah's [body] was never found. They believe that the angels concealed him.

Bani an-Nadir

There was the expedition against Bani an-Nadir (a Jewish tribe). He went out to them on the evening of the Jumu'ah nine days into Rabi' al-Awwal. He returned to them on Tuesday evening and besieged them for twenty-three days.[14] During it the prayer of fear[15] was revealed, and some say that it was during Dhat ar-Riqa'. Some say that the raid on Dhat ar-Riqa' and the prayer of fear were in the fifth year.

The raid on Dhat ar-Riqa' which was called that because of the great number of patches in the banners. He went out after five days of Jumada al-Ula and returned on Wednesday eight days before its end.

Then in Sha'ban he went to the appointed meeting with Abu Sufyan at Badr but met no one.

The Trench or the 'Confederates'

In Shawwal there was the battle of the Trench,[16] which is the battle of the Confederates.[17] Some also say that the Trench was in 5 AH.

Bani Quraydhah

Then there was the raid on Bani Quraydhah.[18] Malik said, "It was in 4 AH." He returned from Quraydhah on the 4th of Dhu'l-Hijjah.

There was the raid[19] which Abu 'Ubaydah ibn al-Jarrah made to the coast, from which he returned without meeting any opposition.

There was also the expedition of Abu 'Ubaydah against Dhat al-Qissah which is on the road to Iraq, but he encountered no opposition.

The Fifth Year of the Hijrah

He sent property and wealth to Quraysh when it reached him that they were experiencing a difficult year.

Some say that the raid on Dhat ar-Riqa' was in it.

Some say that in Sha'ban there was the expedition of al-Muraysi' to Bani al-Mustaliq.

The Trench

Some say that the Trench was in this year. Malik said, "The Trench was four years after the Hijrah, and it happened during intense cold." Malik said, "On that day only four or five were killed as *shuhada'*, and on that day Allah, mighty is He and majestic, revealed, '*When they came at you from above you and from below than you...*" (Surat al-Ahzab 9-11). Quraysh came at them from here, the Jews from here, and the Majd from here", meaning by these last Hawazin.

They say that Dawmat al-Jandal[20] was in the fifth year. He intended to go out against al-Ukaydir in Muharram but he fled and so the Prophet ﷺ returned without encountering any opposition.

In this year he sent 'Abdullah ibn Anees[21] to Sufyan ibn 'Abdillah.

He sent 'Amr ibn Umayyah and his companion to fight Abu Sufyan.

The Messenger of Allah ﷺ sent Ibn Rawahah with thirty mounted men to kill Aysir ibn Razam the Jew.

There was the expedition of Ghalib ibn 'Abdillah[22] upon al-Kadid against Ibn al-Maluh. He returned without encountering any serious opposition.

There was the expedition of Zayd ibn Harithah against Wadi al-Qura' where he met some people from Bani Fazarah and fought them.

There was the second expedition of Zayd against [Fatimah bint Rabi'ah ibn Badr] Umm Qarfah whom he had been ordered to kill. He did not know that he was ordered to kill any other woman, so he defeated them and killed her.

In the days of the new moon of Jumada al-Ula there was the expedition against Bani Lihyan. The Prophet 🌸 went to retaliate for Khubaib ibn 'Adi and his companions. He sent immediately to the smallest of the mountains looking for their dwellings and then they clung to the mountains.

The Messenger of Allah 🌸 sent out small raiding parties.

There was the raid of Abu 'Ubaydah upon Asad and Baliy,[23] from which he returned without having encountered serious opposition.

The Sixth Year of the Hijrah

The ayat of Tayammum

There was the raid upon Bani al-Mustaliq at al-Mursi' which is six or seven days' journey from Madinah, close to Makkah from the direction of al-Juhfah.[24] He put Abaruhum al-Ghifari in charge of Madinah and travelled at the new moon of Sha'ban. The ayah concerning *tayammum* (Surat al-Ma'idah, 6) was revealed then. The Prophet 🌸 killed some of them and took Juwayriyyah bint al-Harith prisoner. Then he freed her and married her.

There were more than seven hundred prisoners. She asked him for them on the night when he took up residence with her and he gave them to her.

'Aishah was accused of indecency and Allah revealed[25] her freedom from wrongdoing.

Al-Hudaybiyyah

There was the expedition of al-Hudaybiyyah. He 繼 went on 'Umrah in Dhu'l-Qa'dah in 6 AH. They put on ihram in Dhu'l-Hulayfah. On the way it reached him that Quraysh were pained at his coming and had sworn an oath that he would not enter Makkah against their wishes. He said 繼 "Mercy on Quraysh! I have not come out to fight them, but I have come out to perform the 'Umrah of this House."

There was all of the contesting of the matter. Then there was the Treaty which was agreed between him and Quraysh for two years. It has also been said that it was for four years, and some say that it was for ten years. He alighted at al-Hudaybiyyah. In it was the Pledge of Allegiance called Ridwan (Good Pleasure)[26] and they were one thousand, four hundred men. Some say they pledged allegiance promising to fight to the death. Others say that they promised not to flee. Some say that he returned 繼 five days before the end of Muharram and that he had remained there about twenty nights. Then he went on the expedition to Khaybar.[27] Others say that he stayed in al-Hudaybiyyah for a month and a half, and yet others that it was for fifty nights.

He sent Bashir ibn Sa'd to the area of Khaybar and he returned without meeting serious opposition.

There was the expedition of Ka'b ibn 'Umayr[28] against Dhat al-Kilah[29] in Syria. He and his companions were killed.

There was the raid of 'Abd ar-Rahman ibn 'Awf on Baliy and Kalb, an area of Syria. Some say that the Messenger of Allah dressed him in a turban with his own hands on the expedition to Dawmat al-Jandal[30] in Sha'ban.

He sent 'Ali ibn Abi Talib to Fadak.[31] He sent 'Abdullah ibn Rawahah with a company of horsemen to come in between 'Ali and Khaybar in order to strike fear into its people. The people of Khaybar came out and so he attacked them in more than ten sudden attacks until he humbled him, then he attacked Bani Sa'd ibn Hudaym.

The Prophet ﷺ created an endowment (waqf)[32] of seven of his date-palm gardens.

He ﷺ performed the prayer for rain because of a drought which affected people.

Umm Ruman, the wife of Abu Bakr, died in Dhu'l-Hijjah, and he ﷺ descended into her grave [to lay the body in place].

The Prophet ﷺ made use of a seal-ring. He only made use of it when he sent an emissary, and someone said to him, "The non-Arabs only read sealed letters" and so he began to make use of one. The inscription on its stone was, "Muhammad is the Messenger of Allah" and some say that it was, "There is no god but Allah, Muhammad is the Messenger of Allah."

The Seventh Year of the Hijrah

Khaybar

In which was the expedition against Khaybar. Malik said, "Khaybar took place six years after the Hijrah." They say, "No one went on it except for the people who had been at al-Hudaybiyyah and a man from Bani Harithah whom he granted permission." He went out in Muharram and put Subay' ibn 'Arfatah al-Ghifari in charge of Madinah. Some also say that it was Abaruhum Kulthum al-Husayn al-Ghifari. They conquered the fortresses of Khaybar which is what Allah, glorious is He, promised at al-Hudaybiyyah in His words, exalted is He, *"And others which you had no power over which Allah has already encompassed."* (Surat al-Fath, 21)

Fadak

There was the matter of Fadak while they were still afraid because of what had been done to Khaybar. Their messengers charged with the task came to Khaybar, or on the way or after they had returned to Madinah, and he made a treaty with them for half the produce of Fadak which he accepted from them. He had not stirred horses or camels for it,[33] and so it was especially for the Prophet ﷺ.

Then he came to Wadi al-Qura'[34] and conquered it and no one in it united against him.

The Messengers sent to the Persians and the Romans

He sent 'Abdullah ibn Hudhafah to Khosroes the emperor of Persia with a letter which he then tore up. The Prophet 🙵 said, "May Allah tear up his kingdom for him."

He sent Dihyah al-Kalbi to Caesar[35] the emperor of the Romans with a letter.[36]

He sent Zayd ibn Harithah with five hundred mounted men against whoever opposed Dihyah.

There was the raid on Dhat as-Salasil close to the road to Syria, in which 'Amr ibn al-'As raided the territory of Bani Sa'd ibn 'Abdillah close to Quda'ah. He asked for help from the Messenger of Allah 🙵 and he helped him. Among those who went out were Abu Bakr and 'Umar and other Muhajirun over whom Abu 'Ubaydah was in charge.

In Dhu'l-Qa'dah the Messenger of Allah 🙵 went out in the same month in which the idolaters had prevented him having access to the Sacred Mosque in Makkah.[37] When he reached Yajij[38] he put down all his weapons and they entered Makkah with only the weapons of riding men: bows and sheathed swords.

The Messenger of Allah 🙵 married Maimunah. In it also was the raid of al-Qadiyyah. He 🙵 alighted in al-Abtah six days into Dhu'l-Qa'dah and stayed with her three days, which is the obligation. Then he travelled on and left Abu Rafi' his freed slave to bring Maimunah to him. He took up residence with her in Sarif[39]. She was the aunt of 'Abdullah ibn 'Abbas. Some say that she was also the aunt of Khalid ibn al-Walid. Her sister was

Umm al-Fadl who was the wife of al-'Abbas ibn 'Abd al-Muttalib. Maimunah entrusted her guardianship to him and he married her to the Messenger of Allah ﷺ. Some also say that he sent Abu Rafi' and another one or two men from the Ansar and that they married her to him.

There was the raid of Zayd ibn Harithah upon at-Tarf to the side of the road to Iraq from which he returned without having met serious opposition.

He sent 'Abdullah ibn Abi Hadrad al-Aslami with two men to the low ground eight miles from Madinah when it reached him that Rufa'ah ibn Qays wanted to unite the tribe of Qays to make war on the Messenger of Allah ﷺ so they laid an ambush for him and Ibn Abi Hadrad shot him with an arrow and killed him.

There also was the raid of Ibn Abi Hadrad on Dhu Khashab.

The Messenger of Allah ﷺ began to use the Mimbar. It has also been said that was in 8 AH. Malik said, "Its wood was from Tamarisk of the forest, and a slave of Sa'd ibn 'Ubadah made it." Someone else said that it was a slave of an Ansari woman, and yet another said that it was a slave of al-'Abbas ibn 'Abd al-Muttalib. He ﷺ gave the khutbah and a tree-trunk besides which he used to stand when giving the khutbah uttered a cry of yearning, so he placed his hand on it and it was still.[40]

The Eighth year of the Hijrah

Mu'tah

There was the expedition to Mu'tah. The Prophet ﷺ sent his forces to Mu'tah in the land of Syria in Jumada al-Ula, and he made Zayd ibn Harithah their Amir. He said, "If he is killed then Ja'far[41] [is the Amir] and if he is killed then 'Abdullah ibn Rawahah [is the Amir]." They encountered Heraclius with his forces which were said to have been one hundred thousand apart from those Arabicised tribes who joined them. They met at a town called Mu'tah. The ones whom the Prophet ﷺ had named were killed and the Muslims agreed upon Khalid ibn al-Walid [as the Amir]. Allah opened the way for him and he killed them and sent a messenger to bring the good news of that to the Messenger of Allah ﷺ. He ﷺ had already told them about that before the messenger's arrival.

The Opening[42] of Makkah

In it was the expedition for the Opening [of Makkah to Islam]. Abu Sufyan had come to the Prophet ﷺ wishing him to extend the term of the truce,[43] but he would not reply to him, and Abu Sufyan returned to Makkah. The Prophet ﷺ made it public knowledge that he wanted to raid Hawazin and so he set out, putting Abaruhum al-Ghifari in charge of Madinah. He repaired to Dhu'l-Hulayfah where al-'Abbas met him. The Prophet ﷺ said to him, "Carry on to Madinah with your household goods." From that place he sent 'Ali ibn Abi Talib to Mushallal in a small raiding party over which he made him amir and he told him to destroy the idol. Then he travelled on ﷺ until he descended on Makkah where he pitched his round tent.

Malik said, "The Messenger of Allah ﷺ went out on the year of the Opening among eight or ten thousand. He concealed his purpose from people so that no one would know where he intended to go. He asked Allah, mighty is He and majestic, to hide that from them." Yahya ibn Sa'id said, "The Prophet ﷺ entered Makkah in the year of the Opening among ten or twelve thousand. He bent his head towards the ground over the prominent front part of his saddle so much that it almost broke," meaning out of humility and gratitude to Allah, "and he said, 'The kingdom belongs to Allah the Overwhelming One'." Malik said, "Makkah was opened on the nineteenth day of Ramadan in the eighth year of the Hijrah, and Khaybar in the sixth year and the Trench was in the fourth year."

They say that in the eighth year the idols were removed from the Ka'bah, those which were in it and which belonged to it, and those idols which were on as-Safa and al-Marwah. In this year the men and women [of Makkah] pledged allegiance over three days.

He sent out small raiding parties from Makkah. He sent Khalid to the people of al-Ghamida'[44]. Then he sent him to the date-palm of al-Yamamah which is a house by a date-palm in which there is a tree and he destroyed it. He came back and he sent him back saying, "Pull it out by its roots."

There was the Smoke[45] and Allah knows best.

Hunayn

In it was the raid on Hunayn.[46] It happened because when he
🕌 decided to go against Makkah to assist Khuza'ah, the news
came to Hawazin that he meant to go against them and so they
prepared for war until they came to the market of Dhu'l-Majaz.
He travelled 🕌 until he overlooked the valley of Hunayn in the
evening before the Sunday. Then he made a treaty with them on
the day of the Sunday in the middle of Shawwal.

He sent out small raiding parties from Hunayn.

There was the raid on at-Ta'if. He turned away when he learnt
that Thaqif were gathering together so he went towards them
and besieged them.[47]

There was the raid on al-Ji'ranah when he had finished with
Hunayn and at-Ta'if. It was at the end of Dhu'l-Qa'dah. Then he
spent the rest of Dhu'l-Qa'dah and Dhu'l-Hijjah in Madinah. 'Itab
ibn 'Usayd led the Hajj. He stood with the Muslims, and the idolaters
remained doing what they used to do in the Age of Ignorance.

The Ninth Year of the Hijrah

In this year people raced with each other to enter Islam.

Musaylimah the Liar[46] wrote a letter to the Messenger of Allah
🕌 and the Messenger of Allah answered him.

Tabuk

In it there was the expedition to Tabuk which is also known as
the "Army of Difficulty". The Prophet 🕌 wrote a letter after the

Opening to the tribes in which Islam had not spread inviting them [to Islam] and he wrote to those in which Islam had spread [calling them] to join an expedition against the Romans and he made an appointment to meet them at Tabuk.[48] He set off at the beginning of Rajab. He put 'Ali ibn Abi Talib in charge of Madinah. Then he reached Tabuk 🌸. Malik said, "The expedition to Tabuk took place in extreme heat." They say that a delegation from the Roman Emperor came to Tabuk and that he sent them back with a reply to their king, and then afterwards sent out many small raiding parties. During this expedition a group of the hypocrites plotted against the Prophet to throw him down from a steep mountain path. Allah revealed to him those ayat about the hypocrites which are in Surat al-Bara'ah (at-Tawbah). Then he mentioned the three who had been left behind.[49]

Surat al-Bara'ah or at-Tawbah

The Messenger of Allah 🌸 returned in Shawwal and sent Abu Bakr to lead the Hajj. After he had gone, Surat al-Bara'ah was revealed and he sent 'Ali ibn Abi Talib with it and told him to announce Bara'ah loudly among people.[50]

Malik said, "The first one to establish the Festival [of the Hajj] for people was Abu Bakr as-Siddiq 🌸 in 9 AH.

The Tenth Year of the Hijrah

The acceptance of Islam of most of the people [of Arabia] was completed so he sent 'Ali to the Yemen, from where he returned without having met serious opposition. He sent Usamah ibn Zayd to ad-Darum in the land of Palestine where he gained spoils and returned safely.

He sent 'Uyaynah ibn Hisn to Bani al-'Anbar inviting them to Islam, but they did not accept so he killed some of them and took others prisoner.

He again sent 'Ali to the Yemen. Some say that he sent him to teach them the fiqh of the *deen*, and some say that he sent him to collect Zakat from the governors and then come to the Messenger of Allah ﷺ during the Farewell Hajj. So 'Ali came to the Messenger of Allah ﷺ in Makkah.

The Farewell Hajj

In it he performed the Farewell Hajj. It is called the Farewell Hajj because he took leave of them. It is also called the Conveying because he said, "Have I conveyed?" It is also called the Hajj of Islam because it is the Hajj in which people's Hajj was completed without there being an idolater among them.

The Eleventh Year of the Hijrah

The Messenger of Allah ﷺ sent Jarir ibn 'Abdillah al-Bajli to Dhu'l-Kila' in the Yemen to invite him to Islam and he became a Muslim. Jarir came back and the Messenger of Allah had died.

He sent Usamah ibn Zayd to Mu'tah in the land of Syria and commanded him to spill blood there but he did not execute the mission before the death of the Messenger of Allah ﷺ and so Abu Bakr [when he became khalifah] commanded him to execute it.

The Death of the Messenger of Allah

In it the Messenger of Allah ﷺ died, may my father and my mother be his ransom ﷺ and show mercy and honour to him, on Monday the twelfth of Rabi' al-Awwal. Ibn 'Uqbah said, "In the house of 'Aishah on her day and upon her bosom when the morning light was strong." Malik said, "He was buried on the Tuesday and people prayed over him individually no one acting as imam." Some say that he was buried when the sun had declined after the midday. Al-'Abbas, 'Ali, al-Fadl ibn 'Abbas and Shuqran, his freed slave, washed him. Some say that this last was called Salih, the freed slave of the Messenger of Allah ﷺ. They went down into his grave. Usamah and Aws ibn Khuli were with them.

His pain ﷺ had begun in the house of Maimunah bint al-Harith on the Wednesday two nights before the end of Safar. Later he was transferred to 'Aishah's house, and he became sick with her until he died. Abu Bakr lead the people in prayer during the sickness of the Messenger of Allah ﷺ for seventeen prayers before his death ﷺ.

Abu Bakr's Khilafah

Allegiance was pledged to Abu Bakr as-Siddiq.

Those of the Arabs who reneged on their allegiance did so.

Abu Bakr ﷺ burnt Ibn al-'Ujah whose name was Iyas ibn 'Abdillah ibn Yalil. That was because he asked Abu Bakr to put him in charge of dealing with those who had reneged and to give him responsibility, which he did. Then he went out and killed Muslims and renegades. Someone wrote [to Abu Bakr about that], and he was captured. Someone said, "He killed him and then burnt him."

He sent Khalid ibn al-Walid against Tulayhah[51] and many of Tulayhah's companions were killed and he fled. Later he accepted Islam and made good his Islam.

The Battle of Yamamah

Then Abu Bakr turned his attention to Musaylimah in al-Yamamah. A woman called Sajah bint al-Harith of Bani Tamim had claimed to be a prophetess and Musaylimah had married her. Some say that Khalid killed Musaylimah and conquered al-Yamamah with a treaty which he made with Muja'ah ibn Mazarah. [In the battle which preceded the treaty] one thousand one hundred of the Muslims died as *shuhada'*, and some say that it was one thousand four hundred seventy of whom had memorised the Qur'an.

Fatimah the daughter of the Messenger of Allah ﷺ died on the third day of Ramadan, when she was twenty-seven years old. That was six months after the Prophet ﷺ and some also say three months, but Malik said, "The former is better established."

Malik said, "Egypt was conquered in 20 AH and Ifriqiyyah (North Africa, particularly what is now Tunisia) on the day of Hafsah's death." Someone else said, "In 27 AH."

Malik said, "Mu'adh ibn Jabal died when he was thirty-two years old. 'Abdullah ibn 'Umar lived to be eighty-seven years of age. 'Umar ibn 'Abd al-'Aziz died when he was forty-two years old," and some say that he was thirty-eight.

Sa'id ibn al-Musayyab[52] was born three years before the end of the khalifate of 'Umar ibn al-Khattab.

Author's Afterword

Abu Muhammad 'Abdullah ibn Abi Zayd said: We have mentioned in this book of our's called *al-Jami'* which we have put at the end of our abridgement [of the *Mudawwanah al-Kubra*] some of that which was been preserved from Malik and from some of his companions and others of those who narrated from the Messenger of Allah ﷺ and from those of our predecessors and imams whom we have mentioned, about courtesy, command and prohibition and other arts. Most of it is from the assemblies of Malik and from his *Muwatta'*.

We have also mentioned something about history and the military expeditions which took place, etc. Some of that is from Malik and some from other people of knowledge.

We have mentioned that which the ummah agree upon in the chapter on the biography [of the Prophet] in this book. We have gathered all of that together with what concision and accuracy is possible for us in discharging that, insha'Allah.

I ask Allah our Lord that He encompass us in His forgiveness and that He benefit us and you by that which He has taught us of His wisdom, and that He realise our hope for the vastness of His mercy, and that He make that which we have simplified of that a blessing for whoever writes it out and a light for whoever learns it.

May Allah bless Muhammad and the family of Muhammad and grant them much peace.

Kitab al-Jami' from the *Mukhtasar* of Abu Muhammad ibn Abi Zayd was completed, may Allah show mercy to him, and by it the entire *Mukhtasar* of *al-Mudawwanah* and *al-Mukhtalitah* was completed, with praise of Allah and by His help, on the sixth of Dhu'l-Qa'dah in 532 AH. (6th July 1138 CE.)

People Mentioned
in the Text

A

Abaruhum al-Ghifari was present at Uhud. He later pledged allegiance under the tree at al-Hudaybiyyah. The Messenger 🌸 put him in charge of Madinah during the 'Umrah which was performed the year after Hudaybiyyah to make up for the one omitted in that year. He was also put in charge of Madinah during the Opening of Makkah.

Al-'Abbas ibn 'Abd al-Muttalib. There is a difference of opinion as to whether he became a Muslim early on and concealed his Islam, or whether he was a latecomer to Islam. He emigrated on the day of the Opening of Makkah.

'Abd al-Malik ibn 'Abd al-'Aziz ibn Jurayj was one of the fuqaha and Qur'an reciters of Makkah. He was one of the very first to compile his knowledge in book form. He died in 150 AH.

'Abd ar-Rahman ibn al-Qasim is one of the most significant of Malik's many illustrious students. Acknowledged by al-Bukhari and an-Nasa'i among others as an incomparable transmitter of hadiths, he devoted nineteen years of his life, until Malik's death, to keeping company with Malik and learning from him. Most importantly he learnt the science of sales and business transactions which Malik went to great lengths to clarify in detail in the *Muwatta'*. When Sahnun questioned him during his compilation of the *Mudawwanah*, a great number of his questions were on the rules of trade and on how to prevent usury from becoming involved in transactions. This makes the *Mudawwanah* along with the *Muwatta'* one of the most significant works for our century. He died in 191/806 at the age of 63.

'Abd al-Wahhab ibn Bukht was an Umayyad mawla of the family of Marwan from Makkah. He lived in Sham and then in Madinah. He narrated from Anas, Abu Hurayrah, Ibn 'Umar, 'Umar ibn 'Abd al-'Aziz and others. He died in 113 AH or 111 AH.

'Abdullah ibn 'Abbas was the cousin of the Prophet 🌸. His mother was Umm al-Fadl. He is the great commentator on the Qur'an. He was still a young man when the Prophet 🌸 died, and so to make up his lack of companionship he exerted himself to learn everything he could from the other older Companions. He soon came to excel many of them in knowledge and at quite an early age he was one of 'Umar's trusted counsellors. He taught many of the most important of the Followers. He died in at-Ta'if in 68 AH.

'Abdullah ibn 'Abd ar-Rahman al-Ansari was one of the people of Madinah and one of their Qadis. Ahmad ibn Hanbal regarded him as trustworthy and many people narrated from him including Malik and al-Awza'i. He died towards the end of the Umayyad period.

187

'Abdullah ibn az-Zubayr ibn al-'Awwam. His mother, Asma bint Abi Bakr, had emigrated while she was pregnant with him and he was the first child born to the Muhajirun in Madinah which caused great joy. He memorised hadith from the Messenger of Allah while he was a boy which he later narrated, just as he narrated from his father, his maternal grandfather, Abu Bakr as-Siddiq, his aunt 'Aishah and others. He was pledged allegiance as Khalifah after the death of Yazid, and all of the Hijaz, Yemen and Iraq agreed to his khalifate. However, Syria and elsewhere had pledged allegiance to 'Abd al-Malik ibn Marwan. Then al-Hajjaj, the general of 'Abd al-Malik, sent an army against him in Makkah. He defended the city for some time but was killed in 73 AH.

'Abdullah ibn Jahsh was one of those who had emigrated to Abyssinia. He was present at Badr. He was the first man to be appointed Amir in Islam. He died as a shaheed in the battle of Uhud.

'Abdullah ibn Mas'ud al-Hudhali fought at Badr and in the other battles. It was he who dealt the death blow to Abu Jahl. He devoted himself to keeping company with the Messenger ﷺ and thus came to narrate many hadiths. He died in 32 AH.

'Abdullah ibn Rawahah was of the Khazraj tribe of the Ansar and had been one of those present at al-'Aqabah. He was one of those who took the Amirate of the army sent to Syria after the death of Zayd ibn al-Harithah until he was himself killed in the same battle of Mu'tah in 8 AH. Khalid ibn al-Walid then took command and retreated with the survivors to Madinah.

Abu 'Amr 'Uthman ibn 'Isa ibn Kinanah was one of the fuqaha of Madinah and a pupil of Malik. He was more disposed to reasoning than to narration of traditions. Malik took him with him for the discussion he held with Abu Yusuf – the pupil of Abu Hanifah and chief Qadi of the Abbasids – in the presence of Harun ar-Rashid. Ibn Kinanah sat in Malik's circle after the death of Malik. He died in approximately 186 AH in Makkah.

Abu Ayyub al-Ansari's name was Khalid ibn Zayd. The Messenger of Allah ﷺ made brotherhood between him and Mus'ab ibn 'Umayr. He died in 52 AH in an army fighting at Constantinople and his tomb is there in Istanbul today where it is visited by Muslims.

Abu'd-Darda was one of the Companions from the Ansar. He had been a trader before Islam and tried to continue with it in Islam but finding that he could not couple it with worship of Allah and reflection, to which he was intensely devoted, he gave it up. He was appointed Qadi in Syria where he died in 31 or 32 AH,

Abu Rafi' "the Copt". Some say that his name was Ibrahim, Aslam, Thabit or Hurmuz. He had belonged to al-'Abbas who gave him to the Prophet who in turn freed him when he gave him the good news that al-'Abbas had become a Muslim. He was present at Uhud and the battles after that. He died in Madinah after the murder of 'Uthman.

Abu 'Ubaydah ibn al-Jarrah was one of the great Companions. He, 'Uthman ibn Madh'un and 'Abd ar-Rahman ibn 'Auf accepted Islam at the same time. The Messenger ﷺ gave him the title of "The Trustee of the Ummah". He was one of the ten Companions with whom the Messenger 🌸 was pleased when he died and to whom he gave the good news of the Garden. He was involved in the conquests in Syria, and died in the plague there in 18 AH.

Abu Murthad al-Ghinawi was a confederate of Hamzah ibn 'Abd al-Muttalib. He died in 12 AH.

'Amir ibn Fuhairah was a freed slave of Abu Bakr and one of the very early people to accept Islam. He had been tortured. It is he who is said, when stabbed in the back with a spear, to have cried out, "I have won! By the Lord of the Ka'bah!" and then to have risen in the air. The man who killed him was so astonished that he could not rest until he found out what he had won. When he discovered that as a shaheed he had immediately entered the Garden, that man himself became a Muslim.

'Amr ibn al-'As accepted Islam at the same time as Khalid ibn al-Walid. He conquered Egypt which he governed under 'Umar, 'Uthman and Mu'awiyah. He died in approximately 42 AH.

'Amr ibn Umayyah accepted Islam as the idolaters returned from Uhud. The Messenger 🌸 sent him as an ambassador to the Negus, the ruler of Abyssinia, and similarly to Abu Sufyan in Makkah with a gift. He died during the Khalifate of Mu'awiyah.

An-Nakha'i. His name was Abu 'Imran Ibrahim. He was the faqih of Iraq in his time and possessed great sincerity, scrupulousness and fine discrimination in the hadiths. An-Nakha'i avoided fame and he would not talk about knowledge unless he was asked. He died in 95 AH when he was still a young man.

Ashhab. He was Abu 'Umar ibn 'Abd al-'Aziz ibn Dawud al-Qaysi al-'Amiri from Egypt. He was one of the leading pupils of Malik. After the death of Ibn al-Qasim he was the leading man of knowledge from the pupils of Malik in Egypt. The hadith narrators who compiled the Sunan books (Abu Dawud, an-Nasa'i and Ibn Majah among others) narrated hadith from him. He was born in 140 AH and died in 204 AH.

Asma' bint Abi Bakr as-Siddiq. She was born twenty-seven years before the Hijrah, and died in 24 AH. She was one of the great women of the Companions whose learning is highly prized by later generations.

'Ata ibn Abi Rabah was a faqih of Makkah from the generation of the Followers. He learnt from Ibn 'Abbas and others. Mujahid, az-Zuhri and al-A'mash learnt from him.

'Ata ibn Yasar was a Qadi from the Followers of Madinah. He learnt from Ibn Mas'ud, Abu Hurayrah, 'Aishah and Maimunah who had freed him from slavery. He was one of the shaykhs of Abu Hanifah. He died in 103 AH, but it has also been said that it was in 94 AH.

Al-Awza'i. His name was 'Abd ar-Rahman ibn 'Umar ibn Abi 'Amr. He was the knowledgeable of the people of Syria in his time of the Sunnah. He was an Imam and there was a sizeable madhhab based around his teaching for some time. He died in 157 AH in Beirut as a murabit, fighting to guard the frontiers of Islam.

Aws ibn Khuli was from Khazraj of the Ansar. He died during the Khalifate of 'Uthman.

D

Dihyah al-Kalbi was one of the great Companions. He was present at Uhud and the battles after that. He was the ambassador of the Messenger of Allah ﷺ to the Roman Emperor Heraclius in 6 AH, who believed in him but, however, whose court did not. Dihyah was a very handsome man and Jibril on some occasions would descend in his form. Dihyah was present at the battle of Yarmuk, and he lived on into the Khilafah of Mu'awiyah ﷺ.

F

Fatimah bint al-Husayn ibn 'Ali ibn Abi Talib. She narrated hadith from her grandmother Fatimah az-Zahra, her father al-Husayn, 'Abdullah ibn 'Abbas and 'Aishah, may Allah be pleased with them

Al-Hajjaj ibn Yusuf ath-Thaqafi was a general and governor at the time of the Umayyads. He is legendary for his ferocity and his willingness to execute anyone who crossed him, but nevertheless he left a diverse inheritance, having seen to the vowelling of the Qur'an and the minting of coins, etc.

Hisham ibn 'Urwah ibn az-Zubayr ibn al-'Awwam of Madinah was one of Malik's shaykhs. He was one of the great memorisers of hadiths in Madinah, and was a man of great caution and virtue. He died in about 146 AH.

I

Ibn Abi Zayd al-Qayrawani, the author of the present book, is widely known as the 'Younger Malik' because of his great knowledge. His most famous work is the astonishing *Risalah* which he wrote in response to a friend's request for a book with which to teach children the *deen* as they are taught the Qur'an. He is said to have written it when he was seventeen years old. In one small volume he taught all the essentials of the *deen*, starting with a crystalline exposition of tawhid, progressing through the five pillars, and all the ordinary transactions of life including marriage and divorce, owning and renting land, business transactions, and concluding with assorted chapters on dress, manners, dreams and visions, etc. He said in his prologue "You have asked me to write a short treatise for you about what is obligatory in the *deen* - those things which should be pronounced by the tongue and believed by the heart and done by the limbs; and about those sunnahs which are associated with these obligatory actions - the confirmed (*mu'akkadah*), the optional (*nafilah*) and the desirable (*raghibah*); something about the courtesies (*adab*) associated with them; along with certain of the key principles and derived judgements in jurisprudence (*fiqh*) according to the madhhab and way of Imam Malik ibn Anas, may Allah have mercy on him; and in addition to mention what the great men of knowledge and fiqh have said about unclear matters in the madhhab in order to make them easier to understand. You have made this request because of your desire to teach these things to children in the same way that you teach them how to read the Qur'an so that they may first of all gain an understanding of the *deen* of Allah and His Shari'ah in their hearts, which will hopefully bring them blessing and a good end result." Ibn Abi Zayd lived under the deviant shi'ah rule of the Fatimids, yet his works contain no polemics against them but a determined restatement of the Islam of the people of Madinah. The present work emerged because Ibn Abi Zayd made an abridgement (*Mukhtasar*) of the *Mudawwanah* of Sahnun. In the tradition of Malik he appended a general book dealing with matters that don't come under any one particular fiqh heading. However, this book has long been published separately in its own right and Ibn Abi Zayd in his own afterword refers to it as an independent work although alluding to its place in his *Mukhtasar*. Most agree that he was born in Qayrawan in 310 AH. He died on the 30th Sha'ban 386 AH/14th September 996 CE.

Ibn Habib was from Cordoba. He was a great and learned 'alim, faqih and scholar of hadith and he became the head of the Malikis in Andalusia after Yahya ibn Yahya, the scholar who transmitted the most widely used version of the *Muwatta'*. He wrote on fiqh, literature and history. One of his best known works is *al-Wadihah*. He died in 238 AH.

Ibn Hazm. He was Muhammad ibn Abi Bakr ibn Muhammad ibn 'Amr al-Hazm al-Ansari. He was the Qadi of Madinah. He narrated from his own father and from Ibn Shihab az-Zuhri. Malik and others narrated from him. An-Nasa'i and Abu Hatim regarded him as a trustworthy narrator of hadiths. He died in

132 AH. He is not to be confused with the later more famous Ibn Hazm of Andalusia.

Ibn 'Ijlan was Muhammad ibn 'Ijlan. He was from Quraysh and born in Madinah. He learnt from his father and from Anas ibn Malik and others. He was trustworthy and narrated many hadiths. He died in 149 AH.

Ibn Mahdi. He was 'Abd ar-Rahman ibn Mahdi ibn Hassan al-'Anbari. He was one of the most learned men on the hadiths and was a trustworthy and dependable memoriser. He was extremely scrupulous. He died in 198 AH.

Ibn Nafi'. He was 'Abdullah ibn Nafi' was one of the muftis of Madinah. He learnt his fiqh from Malik and his peers. He died in 186 AH.

Ibn Shihab az-Zuhri was a Follower from the people of Madinah. Both Abu Hanifah and Malik learnt from him. He is one of the most distinguished names of his generation. He died in 126 AH.

J

Jubayr ibn Mut'im was from Quraysh. He accepted Islam after Hudaybiyyah, but some say during the Opening of Makkah. He died around 57-59 AH.

Juwayriyyah bint al-Harith fell to the lot of Thabit ibn Qays – after the battle of Bani al-Mustaliq – with whom she wrote a contract to purchase her freedom for which she asked the help of the Messenger of Allah. He discharged what she owed in the contract and married her. She died in Madinah in 56 AH, or possibly 50 AH.

K

Ka'b al-Ahbar was from Himyar. He was originally a Jew and accepted Islam and came to Madinah after the death of the Prophet ﷺ during the khalifate of 'Umar, so that he was one of the Followers. He was widely respected by the Companions and is often quoted by later writers. He narrated much from Jewish tradition particularly that which confirmed Islam. He moved to Syria where he died in 32 AH.

Khalid ibn al-Walid was named the 'Sword of Allah' by the Messenger of Allah. He accepted Islam with 'Amr ibn al-'As during the period of truce before the Opening of Makkah. At the battle of Mu'tah when the three amirs designated by the Messenger of Allah had been killed, he took the lead and retrieved the situation. In Abu Bakr's khalifate he led the Muslim armies against the Arabs who reneged on their Islam and against Musaylimah the Liar. Then later he led the armies against the Persians and the Romans with outstanding success. Sayyiduna 'Umar removed him from command because he feared that the Muslims were attributing success in battle to him rather than to the help of Allah. This act of 'Umar has been maliciously misunderstood by lesser men who dare to attribute to him personal jealousy. Khalid faithfully served his replacement Abu 'Ubaydah ibn al-Jarrah. He died in Hims in Syria in 21 AH owning only a slave, his weapons and a horse.

Khubaib ibn 'Adi was of Aws of the Ansar. He was captured by the kuffar and sold in Makkah. Banu al-Harith ibn 'Amir bought him and then killed him because he was the one who had killed al-Harith at the Battle of Badr.

Kulthum ibn al-Hadam was from Aws. He used to live in Quba, and he was known as 'The Companion of the Messenger' ⁂. He accepted Islam before the Messenger's arrival in Madinah, but he was an old man and died a little before Badr. Some say that he was the first of the Companions to die after the Hijrah.

L

Al-Layth ibn Sa'd was the shaykh and man of knowledge of Egypt. He was a great scholar of hadiths and the only one to give fatwa in his time in Egypt. He was born in 93 or 94 AH and so was a contemporary of Malik with whom he had a famous correspondence about the importance of the practice of the people of Madinah, a principle which al-Layth accepted. He died in 165 AH.

M

Maimunah bint al-Harith of the tribe of Hilal. She was the last woman whom the Messenger of Allah ⁂ married. She died in approximately 51 AH at the age of eighty-one.

Malik ibn Anas, the Imam of the Abode of the Hijrah, is "The Imam of the Imams" because he taught Muhammad ibn al-Hasan ash-Shaybani, the Imam of the Hanafi madhhab who narrated a version of the *Muwatta'*, Imam ash-Shafi'i who in turn taught Imam Ahmad ibn Hanbal, and many other Imams of the Sunnah, fiqh and hadiths. Al-Bukhari, Muslim and the other hadiths collectors – the authors of the 'Six Sound Collections' – all transmit the hadiths of the *Muwatta'* except for four hadiths which are unique to him. He was the most strict in his narration of hadiths since, as he said himself, he had never sat with a fool. His *Muwatta'* is the most sahih of the collections of hadiths, yet it is omitted from the 'Six' because it is more than a collection of prophetic hadith and because its hadiths are contained in the other collections. He compiled the *Muwatta'* over forty years and was continually editing and removing material from it so that it would only represent the material which was absolutely agreed upon by the people of Madinah and which would be absolutely necessary for the continuance of the *deen*. It is hard to overestimate the importance of the *Muwatta'*. Shaykh Abdalqadir al-Murabit described it as 'a blueprint for an illuminated city'. The other men of knowledge of his age acknowledged him and felt that he was referred to in the famous hadith saying that "A time will soon come when men beat on the livers of camels seeking knowledge but they will not find any more knowledgeable than the man of knowledge of Madinah." Sufyan ibn 'Uyaynah, his contemporary, said, "We think that it refers to Malik." One of the Abbasid khalifahs asked him to allow the *Muwatta'* to become the official text of the *deen* for the Muslim Ummah, which Malik declined. The significance of this decision was that he distanced himself from becoming an instrument of the empire. He strenuously insisted on the importance of the practice of the people of Madinah of the generations of the Companions, the

Followers and the Followers of the Followers, which he recorded assiduously in his *Muwatta'*. Of great significance to our present age is Malik's exhaustive treatment of the non-usurious trading practices of the people of Madinah, and his analysis of how usury can creep into transactions. This is in the *Book of Sales* of the *Muwatta'* in enormous detail, and in the *Mudawwanah* of Sahnun in even greater detail. Malik is said to have been born in 93/712 and to have died in 179/795.

Ma'n ibn 'Isa al-Madani al-Qazzazi al-Ashja'i was one of the most distinguished of Malik's companions. He died in 98 AH.

Masruq was a faqih of the Followers from the city of Kufa. He learnt from 'Umar, 'Ali, Mu'adh, Ibn Mas'ud and Ubayy. Ibrahim an-Nakha'i and ash-Sha'bi learnt from him. He was one of the worshippers and Qur'an reciters of Kufa. He died in 63 AH.

Al-Miqdad ibn al-Aswad al-Kindi was one of the early ones to accept Islam, and he emigrated in both the emigration to Abyssinia and later to Madinah. He died in 33 AH in the Khalifate of 'Uthman when he was seventy years old.

Mu'adh ibn Jabal was from Khazraj of the Ansar. He was present at the second pledge of al-'Aqabah when he was twenty or twenty-one and was in Badr and all the battles after it. The Messenger ﷺ sent to the Yemen to collect the Zakat and to teach. Anas ibn Malik narrated that the Messenger ﷺ said, "Mu'adh is the most knowledgeable of my community of the halal and the haram." The Messenger died while he was in the Yemen. Later he went on jihad to Syria, where he died in the plague in 18 AH.

Mu'awiyah ibn Abi Sufyan. He accepted Islam at the Opening of Makkah and was later one of those whom the Messenger ﷺ called upon to write down ayat of Qur'an which had been revealed. No surer sign exists of his high standing than that. An attack on his reputation is thus an attack on Qur'an. The fighting that took place between him and Sayyiduna 'Ali, may Allah be pleased with both of them, was because of differing *ijtihad*-judgements that they both felt sufficiently strongly about to go to war. After the murder of 'Ali by the Khawarij who had also attempted to murder Mu'awiyah, al-Hasan ibn 'Ali relinquished the khalifate to Mu'awiyah in order to spare the blood of the Muslims. Sayyiduna Mu'awiyah then ruled wisely and nobly for a considerable time, a period in which the Muslims were undivided and victorious over their enemies. Qadi 'Iyad said, "For us he is the fifth of the Rightly Guided Khulafa." He died in 60 AH.

Muhammad ibn 'Abdillah ibn 'Abd al-Hakam. A noted man of knowledge who was the leading scholar in the tradition of Malik in Egypt in his time. People travelled from afar to study with him and he wrote a number of works. He died in 268 AH.

Muhammad ibn 'Abdillah ibn 'Abd ar-Rahim ibn Sa'id ibn Abi Zur'ah al-Masri 'al-Barqi'. He was a trustworthy narrator of hadith and he transmitted the *Sirah* of Ibn Hisham. He died in 249 AH.

Muhammad ibn Maslamah was one of the great Companions from the Ansar. The Prophet ﷺ appointed him as his khalifah over Madinah during some of the expeditions. He made brotherhood between him and Abu 'Ubaydah ibn al-Jarrah who was one of the ten promised the Garden. He died around the year 43 AH when he was seventy-seven years old.

Muhammad ibn al-Munkadir was a Follower who learnt from Ibn 'Umar, Ibn 'Abbas, 'Aishah and others. He was one of Malik's shaykhs. He died in 131 AH at the age of seventy-six years of age.

Mujahid was a hafidh and teacher of Qur'an and a commentator. Ibn 'Abbas taught him the Qur'an. He also learnt from 'Aishah, Umm Hani', Abu Hurayrah and others. He died in 103 AH at 83 years of age.

Musa ibn Maysurah. Malik narrated from him, and an-Nasa'i regarded him as trustworthy.

Musa ibn 'Uqbah ibn Abi 'Ayyash. Born in Madinah where he died in 141 AH. He was of the generation of the Followers, and met a number of Companions, among them Ibn 'Umar, Anas and Jabir. He compiled a work on *sirah* and military expeditions, which Malik regarded as the soundest work on the matter. The book does not survive but because considerable portions were transmitted by other authors, it has largely been reconstructed.

Musaylimah al-Kadhdhab "the Liar" was called Maslamah. In his infamous letter, he wrote "from Maslamah the messenger of Allah to Muhammad the Messenger of Allah, let us divide the land between us," to which the Messenger of Allah ﷺ replied, "From Muhammad the Messenger of Allah to

Musaylimah (lit. 'Little Maslamah') the Liar, the land belongs to Allah and He causes whomever He wills to inherit it." The Muslims under the Khalifah Abu Bakr ؓ fought and killed Musaylimah and many of his followers at al-Yamamah. Many of the Companions were killed, including a great number who had memorised the Qur'an. It was this which inspired 'Umar to insist on the compilation of the Qur'an.

N

Nafi' ibn Abi Nu'aym the Qur'an reciter (al-Qari') who died about ten years before Malik whom he taught Qur'an. This is the man of whom Malik said, "The recitation of Nafi' is Sunnah." His recitation, which was considered by the Followers of the people of Madinah to transmit their recitation, was in turn transmitted mainly by two men of knowledge, Warsh and Qalun, whose recitations spread in North Africa.

Nafi' ibn Sarjis Abu 'Abdullah ad-Daylami became one of the key teachers among the Followers in Madinah. Abu Hanifah, Malik and al-Layth all learnt from him. Al-Bukhari said that the *isnad*, "Malik from Nafi' from Ibn 'Umar", from the Messenger of Allah ﷺ is "the golden chain of authority". He died in 120 AH

Q

Al-Qasim ibn Muhammad ibn Abi Bakr as-Siddiq was Madinan. He learnt from his aunt 'Aishah and Ibn 'Abbas and others. He died in 106 or 107 AH.

R

Rabi'ah ar-Ra'y was Rabi'ah ibn Farrukh at-Taymi. He was one of the main teachers of Malik. He had learnt from Anas, as-Sa'ib ibn Yazid and Ibn al-Musayyab. He died in 136 AH. In the text he is most often mentioned simply as Rabi'ah.

Ar-Rabi' ibn Khuthaim was from Kufa. He was a Follower who learnt from Ibn Mas'ud and others. His son 'Abdullah, ash-Sha'bi and Ibrahim an-Nakha'i narrated from him. He died in either 61 or 63 AH.

S

Sa'd ibn Khaythamah was a chief of Aws of the Ansar, he died in battle in Badr.

Sa'd ibn 'Ubadah was the chief of Khazraj who was one of the people of Madinah at the Pledge of 'Aqabah before the Hijrah. He died in Sham in 15 AH.

Sahnun. His name was Abu Sa'id 'Abd as-Salam Sahnun ibn Sa'id ibn Habib at-Tanukhi. He was from Qayrawan. Poverty prevented him from travelling to Madinah to learn from Malik. However, after Malik's death he travelled to Egypt to study with one of Malik's main pupils, 'Abd ar-Rahman ibn al-Qasim, and the *Mudawwanah* is his record of what he learnt from Ibn al-Qasim as well as from Ibn Wahb and others. The *Mudawwanah* soon became an indispensable reference for those who want to follow the practice of the people of Madinah and to deepen in knowledge of Malik's way. However, the *Mudawwanah* is a lengthy work and so many scholars worked on abridging it and producing *Mukhtasar* (abridgement) works from it, among whom was the author of this book, Ibn Abi Zayd al-Qayrawani. He appended the present book to that abridgement, but however it has always existed as an independent work in its own right. Sahnun died in 240 AH. His son Abu 'Abdullah Muhammad ibn Sahnun was also a noted faqih and scholar. He died in 255 AH.

Sa'id ibn Abi Hind was the freed slave of Samurah and narrated from Ibn 'Abbas, Abu Hurayrah and a number of other people. He died in the beginning of the Khilafah of Hisham, one of the Umayyads.

Sa'id ibn Jubayr was a notable Imam. He would recite the entire Qur'an every two nights. Many narrated from him. Al-Hajjaj killed him in 95 AH.

Sa'id ibn al-Musayyab al-Makhzumi was one of the Seven Fuqaha' of Madinah in the time of the Followers. 'Ali ibn al-Madini said, "I don't know of any of the Followers who was vaster in knowledge than Sa'id. For me he is the most majestic of the Followers." There is disagreement as to the year of his death, but the most likely date is 94 AH.

Sahl ibn Hanif was one of the Ansar and had been present at Badr and Uhud. Many learnt from him of whom there was Abu Layla. He died in 38 AH in Kufa and 'Ali ibn Abi Talib prayed over him.

Sakinah bint al-Husayn ibn 'Ali ibn Abi Talib. Her name was actually Aminah or Ameenah, or possibly Amimah. Sakinah –

"Tranquillity" – was a name given to her by her mother. She was a very literate woman to whom the poets often went for judgement on their poetry. She died in Madinah in 117 AH, but it has also been said that it was in Makkah in 126 AH.

Salim ibn 'Abdillah was the grandson of 'Umar ibn al-Khattab. He learnt from his father 'Abdullah and from Abu Hurayrah. He taught his own son Abu Bakr, and az-Zuhri and Nafi'. He died in 106 AH.

Shuqran was an Abyssinian called Salih ibn 'Adi, and some say that the Messenger of Allah ﷺ inherited him from his father. It has also been said that he was Persian. Someone else said that he had belonged to 'Abd ar-Rahman ibn 'Awf and that he had given him to the Prophet ﷺ. Some say that he lived in Madinah after the death of the Prophet, but it is also said that he had a house in Basrah.

T

Tamim ad-Dari resided in Madinah and later moved to Jerusalem after 'Uthman was killed. He died in 40 AH.

U

'Umar ibn al-Khattab ﷺ was the second of the Khulafa ar-Rashidun. He mentioned one day to the Companions that it had occurred to him to record the Sunnah just as the Qur'an had been compiled and written down. Not one of the Companions objected and all of them approved. However, 'Umar continued to ask for Allah's guidance by means of the supplication of *istikharah* for almost a month. He then reconsidered his original idea because he realised that the People of the Book had done the same thing, and mixed the material thus recorded with the revelations granted to their prophets, and that was one of the reasons they had gone astray.

'Umar ibn 'Abd al-'Aziz is the well known right-acting Umayyad khalifah. He served a period as governor of Madinah where he learnt the fiqh and practice of the people of Madinah, which he was to put to such good use as khalifah. He wrote to the people of knowledge such as Hasan al-Basri for their advice on matters which he faced and also commanding them to write down what they knew of the Sunnah. Thus it was that he initiated the recording of the Sunnah and the fiqh. Of the books written at his command, Malik's *Muwatta'* is the earliest to have survived. He died in 101 AH.

Umm al-Fadl was Lubabah bint al-Harith of the tribe of Hilal was the wife of al-'Abbas. She accepted Islam in Makkah after as-Sayyidah Khadijah and then emigrated to Madinah after the Islam of al-'Abbas was made public. She died during the khalifate of 'Uthman.

Umm 'Atiyyah Nusaybah bint al-Harith – she was one of the great women Companions. She went on a number of expeditions with the Messenger of Allah ﷺ and took part in his defence at Uhud. She also treated the sick and wounded. A number of the Companions and Followers in Basrah learnt how to wash the dead from her. It has been said that she was called Nusaybah bint Ka'b of the Ansar.

Umm Ruman Zaynab bint 'Amir the wife of Abu Bakr as-Siddiq. She was the mother of 'Aishah and 'Abd ar-Rahman.

'Urwah ibn az-Zubayr ibn al-'Awwam. He narrated from his father az-Zubayr, his brother 'Abdullah, his mother Asma' bint Abi Bakr, his aunt 'Aishah, 'Ali ibn Abi Talib and others. He was a faqih and a man of great standing. He died after 90 AH.

Usamah ibn Zayd ibn Harithah was the son of Zayd who was the freed slave of the Messenger ﷺ. He was born in Islam and was twenty years old when the Messenger ﷺ died. Just before his death, the Prophet had put him in charge of a great army which was to fight the Romans in Syria. Under his command were men such as Abu Bakr and 'Umar who were much older and whose high standing was unquestioned. However, the Messenger ﷺ died before the army set off, and many of the companions wanted to rescind the command, especially since a great number of the Arabs reneged on their Islam or refused to pay the Zakat and thus posed a threat to Madinah and ultimately to the future of Islam. Abu Bakr ﷺ refused to rescind an order given by the Messenger of Allah. The effect of the army's setting out was to convince the tribes that the people of Madinah must have great reserve forces if they could afford to send an army to attack the Roman Empire at such a moment. It thus deterred an Arab attack on Madinah. Usamah died in Madinah in 54 AH.

'Uthman ibn Talhah ibn Abi Talhah was from Quraysh. On the Day of the Opening of Makkah the Messenger ﷺ gave him and his two cousins, the sons of Shaybah ibn 'Uthman ibn Abi Talhah, the keys of the Ka'bah as a perpetual trust. He resided in Makkah after the death of the Messenger ﷺ dying himself in 42 AH. It has been said that he died as a shaheed on the day of *al-Ajnadayn.*

Z

Zayd ibn Aslam was the freed slave of 'Umar ibn al-Khattab. His father was one of the captives taken at 'Ayn at-Tamr, and he accepted Islam. Zayd is counted as one of the most trustworthy of the people of Madinah and one of their learned and knowledgeable worshippers.

Zayd ibn Harithah was the most famous freed slave of the Messenger ﷺ. He had been enslaved in the age of Ignorance, and Hakeem ibn Hazzam bought him for his aunt Khadijah who in turn gave him to her husband ﷺ. The Messenger ﷺ made him the amir over an army which went to Syria and he was killed at Mu'tah in 8 AH.

Zaynab bint Khuzaymah, the wife of the Messenger ﷺ was named "The Mother of the Bereft" because she was one of the most compassionate of women towards the poor and the bereft in both the Age of Ignorance and Islam. She only remained with the Messenger ﷺ two or three months and then died at thirty years of age or so.

Ziyad ibn Abi Ziyad Maysurah al-Makhzumi of Madinah was the freed slave of 'Abdullah ibn 'Ayyash ibn Abi Rabi'ah. He was trustworthy and a worshipper who did without the world. 'Umar ibn 'Abd al-'Aziz used to honour him. He died in 135 AH.

ঞ

In these brief biographical sketches it is all too easy to give the impression of dry scholars removed from the realities of everyday life in their narration of fiqh and hadiths. These men and women lived their lives in the world as others do, in market places, in wealth and in poverty, and many of them lived and died in battle, worshipping Allah day and night. Malik's slavegirl told Ibn al-Qasim that for many years Malik had done the prayer of fajr with the *wudu'* of 'Isha.

There is a glimpse of the enormous spiritual stature of these men and women in Qadi 'Iyad's *Tartib al-Madarik*, some of which Aisha Bewley has translated and put on her invaluable homepage.

Further Reading

Al-Muwatta' by Imam Malik, translated by Aisha Bewley. This incomparable work has fittingly received a translation and editing worthy of it, resulting in a classic Islamic work in the English language. This is the work whose authenticity is unquestioned because of the impeccable credentials of Imam Malik both as a narrator of hadiths and as Imam of the Sunnah. Published in a bi-lingual edition by Diwan Press.

Ash-Shifa by Qadi 'Iyad, translated by Aisha Bewley and published as *Muhammad the Messenger of Allah* by Diwan Press. From deep within the tradition of the fuqaha of the people of Madinah, Qadi 'Iyad wrote this masterful and deeply moving portrait of the Messenger ﷺ. It has always been recognised by the Muslims as the leading work in this field.

Al-Mudawwanah al-Kubra by Sahnun is as yet untranslated in its entirety. It is significant that less than a quarter of it is taken up with the five pillars of Islam. The rest is a detailed exposition of the cases which arise in the ordinary transactions of life, the *mu'amalat*, such as trade, marriage, divorce, inheritance, etc.

Mukhtasar Khalil is the most famous 'abridgement' of the above.

Root Islamic Education by Shaykh Abdalqadir as-Sufi. Published by Madinah Press. The seminal work by Shaykh Abdalqadir which restates the argument for the importance of the practice of the people of Madinah and thus the importance of Imam Malik ibn Anas and the people who transmitted from him.

Al-'Awasim min al-Qawasim by Qadi Abu Bakr ibn al-'Arabi. This is the most outstanding work on the *Fitnat al-Kubra*. It illuminates the clashes between the parties according to the issues of fiqh involved. This remarkable work has been translated by Aisha Bewley as *Defence Against Disaster*. Published by Diwan Press.

Al-Qawanin al-Fiqhiyyah by Ibn Juzayy al-Kalbi. A work of *muqaranah* in which the author details with absolute clarity not only the clear position of the people of Madinah but divergent views within the Maliki madhhab and from the other schools. Translated by Dr. Asadullah Yate and published by Diwan Press.

Kitab at-Tashil li 'Uloom at-Tanzil by Ibn Juzayy al-Kalbi. A compendious tafsir which yet manages to remain within the limits of one single Arabic volume. Unusually it spans both crystal clear *shari'* judgement and lucid exposition of spiritual knowledge. As yet unpublished.

Ar-Risalah by Ibn Abi Zayd al-Qayrawani. Translated by Aisha Bewley and published by Diwan Press.

Bidayat al-Mujtahid wa Nihayat al-Muqtasid by Abu-l-Walid Muhammad ibn Ahmad ibn Rush al-Hafid (Averroes) (d. 595/1198). Although primarily known in the West as the commentator on Aristotle and thus responsible for the great impulse given to Western philosophy by Muslim thinkers, Ibn Rushd was also an important Maliki qadi and faqih. This is his masterwork. He examined all the derivative rulings of the shari'ah and the differences among the fuqaha' within the Maliki school and in the other madhhabs and relates them to the principles of fiqh. Published in hardback in two volumes as *The Distinguished Jurist's Primer.* Translated by I. Nyazee.

A Glossary of Islamic Terms, Aisha Bewley, Ta-Ha Publishing Ltd., London, 1998. This indispensable resource, as well as containing an encyclopaedic lexicon of terms arranged according to subject matter and covering all schools of thought, has very concise biographical material on a huge number of salihun and people of knowledge.

The Origins of Islamic Law: The Qur'an, the Muwatta' and Madinan 'Amal by Dr. Yasin Dutton. This book considers the methods used by Malik in the *Muwatta'* to derive judgements of the law from the Qur'an and is thus concerned on one level with the finer details of Qur'anic interpretation. However, since any discussion of the Qur'an in this context must also include consideration of the Sunnah this latter concept, especially its relationship to the terms hadith and *'amal* ('traditions' and 'living tradition'), also receives considerable attention. The book is the first to question the hitherto accepted frameworks of both the classical Muslim view and the current revisionist Western view on the development of Islamic law. It is also the first study in a European language to deal specifically with early development of the Madinan, later Maliki, school of jurisprudence, as it is also the first to demonstrate in detail the various methods used, both linguistic and otherwise, in interpreting the legal verses of the Qur'an. Curzon Press, 1999, ISBN 0-7007-1062-0.

'Amal v Hadith in Islamic Law, "Islamic Law and Society" Vol.3, No.1 (1996), pp. 13-40, by Dr. Yasin Dutton

ENDNOTES

CHAPTER 1

1 Malik ibn Anas in the *Muwatta'*.

2 Ahmad narrated this hadith in a different wording in his *Musnad*.

3 *Ahwa'* means whims, caprices and desires, but is here translated as 'erroneous opinions'. It is the plural of *hawa'* which can also mean love. It is often coupled with *shahwah* pl. *shahawat*, which denotes appetites.

4 Ibn Majah narrated the meaning of this hadith in a different wording from Abu Hurayrah.

5 The Khawarij seceded from both Sayyiduna 'Ali and Sayyiduna Mu'awiyah 🙏, both of whom they tried to murder succeeding only with the former. Among their *bid'ah* was that they counted any Muslim of wrong action a disbeliever.

6 From the hadith of Abu Sa'id in the *Muwatta'*.

7 The Qadariyyah are those who propound the free-will of man as opposed to predestination and the decree of Allah.

8 The Murji'ah are those who say that only faith in the heart matters, as opposed to action. They are thus willing to overlook serious wrong action.

9 The Rafidah are the 'Rejectors' i.e. the Shi'ah, because they reject the khalifates of the first three khulafa'.

10 As narrated by Abu Hurayrah in the hadith transmitted by Ibn Majah.

11 "Aboveness is an expression for the fact that a thing is higher than another, and is used literally about bodies such as when you say, 'Zayd is on (*fawq*) the roof,' but used metaphorically for meanings, such as when you say, 'The master is superior to (*fawq*) his slave.' The aboveness of Allah, exalted is He, over His '*arsh* is in the sense of a meaning, by which is meant in terms of honour, and it is in the sense of rule and kingship, and it refers to the meaning of control." 'Ali ibn Khalaf al-Manufi al-Maliki al-Misri, *Kifayat at-talib ar-rabbani*

12 "The '*arsh* is a luminous physical entity which encompasses all physical entities, whose reality we cannot categorically detail. It is the first of all created things, according to the most correct view, and is above the heavens. The *kursi* is beneath it between its legs. Linguistically it refers to every thing that is high." Ahmad ibn Ghanim an-Nafrawi, *al-Fawakih ad-dawani 'ala Risalah Ibn Abi Zayd al-Qayrawani*

13 See a hadith narrated by Jabir in *Sunan Ibn Majah*.

14 "*Faces on that Day will be bright, towards their Lord gazing*" Surat al-Qiyamah, 23

15 It can also mean that he saw some or one of the greatest signs of his Lord. The reference is to Surat an-Najm, 18.

16 It is noteworthy that in this work as in many other works of '*aqidah* the author does not mention the Mahdi as a significant sign of the Hour. That reflects the fact that few of the narrations about the Mahdi are dependable, as Ibn Khaldun demonstrated, although the sheer volume of them compensates somewhat for their individual weakness.

17 The people of Madinah and most of the people of the Sunnah read the above ayah as, "*No one knows its interpretation but Allah. And those firmly*

established in knowledge say, 'We believe in it, all is from our Lord'." However, some, among them Ibn Rushd the author of *Bidayat al-Mujtahid*, read it as, "*No one knows its interpretation but Allah and those firmly established in knowledge…*" – Trans.

18 *Sahih al-Bukhari.*

19 *Sahih Muslim*

20 Ibn 'Adi narrated it in a number of versions which are all weak but the very number of different narrations lends it some authenticity.

21 Malik's position in this is a clear example of the position of all of the salaf and thus has been espoused by all the people of the Sunnah since. From this it is clear that those who even delve into discussing the matter at all have thus entered into innovation.

22 The hadith of 'descent' is the famous hadith which mentions that in the last third of the night Allah descends to the lower heaven.

23 The Haruriyyah are a sect of the Khawarij who considered a Muslim to be a kafir when he does a wrong action.

24 The Ibadiyyah are another and more moderate sect of the Khawarij who are extant today in Oman and parts of Algeria.

25 Subaigh came to Madinah and began to ask people about the ambivalent ayats of the Qur'an. 'Umar beat him, and ordered Muslims not to sit with him.

26 This is not licence for internecine warfare between groups each of which claims that it is orthodox and that its opponents are innovators, etc. This is the position for a genuine Muslim ruler governing by the Sunnah when confronted by heretical sects.

CHAPTER 2

1   She, however, is the aforementioned Juwayriyyah 🌿 who had been known as Barrah.

CHAPTER 3

1   The *sa'* is four *mudd*s. The *mudd* is the measure of what two cupped hands can contain. However, it and the *sa'* have specific volumetric sizes, and the people of Madinah had vessels from the time of the Prophet 🌿 of the defined sizes of the *mudd* and the *sa'*

2   *Al-maqsurah* is the area around the qiblah, which in many mosques was fenced off to protect the Amir when he led the prayer, some say from after the time of the murder of 'Umar.

3   Fadak is an oasis in the north of the Hijaz inhabited then by some Jewish tribes.

4   Traders from people of the dhimmah are allowed to come on trade to Madinah for a maximum of three days. Elsewhere in the Arabian Peninsula apart from Makkah they may stay longer although they may not reside.

5   The *sadaqat* (*awqaf*) were plots of land in and around Khaybar that were a part of the Prophet's fifth from the booty, which were not inherited at his death by his family.

CHAPTER 4

1   Hadiths are texts and Sunnah is practice. See Dutton, Yasin: "'Amal v Hadith in Islamic Law", Islamic Law and Society Vol.3, No.1 (1996), pp. 13-40. See also Shaykh Abdalqadir as-Sufi's *Root Islamic Education* which draws very largely on the writings of Qadi 'Iyad, particularly his *Tartib al-Madarik*.

2 This statement is not an affirmation of the sovereignty of the people. The 'people' here are the people of Madinah of the generations of the Companions, the Followers and the Followers of the Followers, and particularly their people of knowledge and fuqaha', who transmitted the Sunnah of the Prophet 🕮 in practice as well as with hadiths.

3 *Su'al* means both to ask a question and to ask for something.

4 Transmission of hadiths from the writing of a man of knowledge which he has written with his own hand and which he has said he heard directly from so-and-so and which he permits the student to narrate.

5 Transmitting his hadiths with his permission.

CHAPTER 5

1 The place some way from Madinah where Abu Dharr withdrew and where he died.

2 In the month of Dhu'l-Hijjah 63 AH, Yazid ibn Mu'awiyah permitted the army of Sham under the command of Muslim ibn 'Uqbah al-Murri to attack Madinah.

1 Ad-Dawraqi, at-Tabari

2 at-Tabarani

3 At-Tirmidhi

4 At-Tirmidhi

5 Abu Dawud

6 At-Tabarani

7 A similar hadith is to be found in *Sunan an-Nasa'i.*

8 Abu Dawud, an-Nasa'i and Ibn 'Asakir

9 *Sunan Ibn Majah*

10 Narrated by Muslim in these words.

11 The dialect of Quraysh did not use the hamzah a great deal. This is retained more in the recitation of Nafiʿ through Imam Warsh and Imam Qalun, which is called the 'recitation of ease' since there are fewer hamzahs. Nafiʿ was the Imam in Qur'an recitation of Madinah, and Malik said, "The recitation of Nafiʿ is sunnah." As to the use of hamzah when it is recited, Abu Muhammad Makki ibn Abi Talib said, "One should pronounce the hamzah with the breath easily," meaning not with a constriction of the larynx and a forced guttural sound.

12 It cannot escape the reader that this is a statement which is clearly applicable to some performance recitations commonly and mistakenly called *tajweed*. This latter term, which is an obligation of Qur'an recitation as much as the reciter is able, means to articulate all of the letters of the recitation clearly and accurately as well as the vowels, observing doubled letters and the long and short vowels; it does not mean the elaborate singing, and all of the ritual that has come to accompany it, of a growing number of paid reciters and recording artists.

13 Some disapprove of writing the names of the surahs and the number of their ayats at their beginnings, for example, ʿAbdullah ibn Masʿud who said, "Do not mix anything with the Book of Allah which is not from it." ʿAbdullah ibn ʿUmar and a group of the Followers disapproved of writing diacritical points and vowels in the *mushaf*. Rabiʾah ibn Abi ʿAbd ar-Rahman and others licensed it as a concession. Note the balance in Malik's position. He saw no harm in it for learning Qur'an, but wanted source, reference copies and Qur'an reciters' copies of the *mushaf* to be identical to those which ʿUthman 🌺 had written.

14 Just as one follows the original *mushafs* in every detail one should copy them in their spelling as well.

15 'Numbered Days' is a name for the three days of Mina after the sacrifice of 'Eid al-Adha during which the Sunnah is to say openly, "Allahu Akbar" and "La ilaha illa'llah" and do dhikr for the sake of Allah.

16 The 'Known Days' are the day of sacrifice itself and the two days afterwards in which the sacrificial animals are slaughtered.

CHAPTER 6

1 *Sahih al-Bukhari*

2 *Muwatta'* and *Jami' at-Tirmidhi*

3 Malik narrated it in the *Muwatta'*, and at-Tirmidhi in his *Jami'*. It is one of the forty hadith of an-Nawawi.

4 Narrated by Malik in *Muwatta'* as part of a longer tradition.

5 Malik narrated it in the *Muwatta'*, and Ibn Majah in a slightly different wording.

6 *Sahih al-Bukhari*, *Jami' at-Tirmidhi* and *Sunan Abu Dawud*.

7 The last piece of advice which the Messenger of Allah ﷺ gave to Mu'adh as he sat on his mount on his way to the Yemen at the command of the Messenger. It is narrated slightly differently in the *Muwatta'*. Ahmad, at-Tirmidhi and others narrate versions which confirm its meaning.

8 Malik in the *Muwatta'*. There are versions in *Sahih al-Bukhari* and *Sahih Muslim*.

9 Malik in the *Muwatta'*.

10 Surah Ali 'Imran, 159. And He said, mighty is He and majestic, '*So say to him gentle words*'." (Surah Ta Ha, 44. The two who are commanded are Musa and Harun, who are ordered to speak gently to Fir'awn. This is a

Qur'anic indication of how Muslims must approach people in authority even unbelievers.

11 *Jami' at-Tirmidhi* and *Sunan Ibn Majah.*

12 A similar hadith is narrated by Ahmad.

13 *Sahih Muslim* and *Jami' at-Tirmidhi*

14 *Jami' at-Tirmidhi* and *Musnad Ahmad.*

CHAPTER 7

1 Malik in *Muwatta'*

2 *Sahih al-Bukhari*

3 *Sahih al-Bukhari, Sahih Muslim, Sunan Abu Dawud* and *Jami' at-Tirmidhi.*

4 The meaning is confirmed by a hadith in *Sahih al-Bukhari.*

5 Malik in the *Muwatta', Sahih Muslim, Jami' at-Tirmidhi* and *Musnad Ahmad.*

6 Malik in *Muwatta', Sahih Muslim, Sunan Abu Dawud, Jami' at-Tirmidhi, Sunan an-Nasa'i,* and *Musnad Ahmad.*

CHAPTER 8

1 i.e. matters which are perfectly halal which he would avoid doing, although not considering them haram. One of the principles of fiqh is *sadd adh-dhara'i,* which means that whatever leads to something that is haram should be avoided even though it might appear to be halal in itself.

2 Malik in the *Muwatta'*

3 Malik in the *Muwatta'*

4 *Sahih Muslim*

5 A variant of a hadith narrated by Malik in the *Muwatta'.*

6 "It has two rewards: the reward for [treating one's] relatives [well] and the reward for sadaqah." *Sahih al-Bukhari.*

7   Malik in the *Muwatta'*

8   The hadith of al-Mughirah ibn Shu'bah 🙵 that he said, "The Messenger of Allah 🙵 said, 'Allah disapproves of three things for you: "it was said and he said" (i.e. tittle-tattle), asking many questions, and squandering wealth'." *Musnad Ahmad*

9   A hadith of the Messenger 🙵 narrated by at-Tirmidhi and Ahmad. It is hadith No. 11 of the forty hadiths of Imam an-Nawawi.

10 *Sahih al-Bukhari, Sahih Muslim* and *Sunan Abu Dawud.*

11 Whereas the wealth of those who forcibly expropriate people's wealth is haram.

12 In the *Mudawwanah* Ibn al-Qasim said, "Malik disapproved of Christians being in the Muslims' markets because of their transacting with usury and regarding it as permissible. He thought they should leave the markets."

CHAPTER 10

1   *Sahih al-Bukhari, Sunan Abu Dawud, Sunan an-Nasa'i, Sunan Ibn Majah* and *Musnad Ahmad.*

2   'Abdullah ibn 'Umar said, "The Messenger of Allah 🙵 said, 'When one of the Jews greets you he only says, "*as-samu 'alaikum* – death to you" so say, "*alaika* – upon you".'" *Muwatta'*.

3   Malik in the *Muwatta', Sunan Abu Dawud, Jami' at-Tirmidhi, Sunan Ibn Majah* and *Musnad Ahmad.*

4   Malik, *Sahih al-Bukhari, Sahih Muslim, Sunan Abu Dawud, Jami' at-Tirmidhi* and *Musnad Ahmad.*

5   i.e. that is sufficient to show that he has discontinued shunning him.

6   literally a "grey haired" Muslim.

7   A reference to His words, exalted is He, *"On a day when mankind stand for the Lord of the Worlds."* Surat al-Muttaffifin, 6.

8   A hadith with the same meaning but a slightly different wording is in *Jami' at-Tirmidhi*.

9   Literally "the lands of the blacks", which encompasses some of Upper Egypt, present-day Sudan, northern Nigeria, Niger, and Mali, etc.

10 Surat al-Isra, 23

11 Surat al-Isra, 24

CHAPTER 11

1   Surat al-Baqarah, 124

2   Malik in the *Muwatta'*.

3   Malik in the *Muwatta'*.

4   Many hadiths are narrated on the virtues of cupping, e.g.: "It is a healing and a blessing, and it increases intelligence and memory." *Sunan Ibn Majah*. "The best of what I use for treatment is cupping," *Sahih al-Bukhari* and *Sahih Muslim*. "No assembly of angels passed by me without saying, 'You must use cupping'." *Jami' at-Tirmidhi, Sunan Ibn Majah* and *Musnad Ahmad*. "If there is good in anything of that with which you treat yourselves, then it is in cupping." *Musnad Ahmad*.

5   *Khitmi* – althæa officinalis

6   A fortress on the borders of Dar al-Islam to which Muslim men went to protect the Muslims from their enemies, spending time in training, dhikr and study, as well as in active service.

7   *Katam* is a dye-plant which has a red colour and which is mixed with *wasmah* – either indigo or woad – to dye hands and hair.

8   Kohl is a preparation, traditionally of Antimony, used to darken around the eyes. Often used medicinally, it is also a cosmetic. Some preparations sold today are poisonous.

9   The traditional female circumcision of the Muslims must not be confused with the female genital mutilation that is widespread in parts of Africa known as Pharaonic circumcision. The former is a very minor operation involving no damage to the woman when carried out by suitably qualified practitioners. The latter is a particularly abhorrent mutilation.

CHAPTER 12

1   *"O Prophet! Tell your wives and daughters and the believing women to draw their outer garments closely around themselves. That makes it more likely that they will be recognised and not harmed. Allah is All-Forgiving, Most Merciful."* Surat al-Ahzab, 59.

2   Cloths of wool, wool mixed with silk or linen which had been used as waistwrapper garments for the lower half of the body.

3   *"O you who believe! Those you own as slaves and those of you who have not yet reached puberty should ask your permission to enter at three times: before the dawn prayer and when you have undressed at noon and after the night prayer – three times of nakedness for you."* Surat an-Nur, 56.

4   A reference to *"Those who guard their private parts except from their spouses or those they own as slaves."* Surat al-Muminun, 5-6

5   It is forbidden to castrate humans. The appearance of eunuchs in this chapter is because tribal peoples humiliated their defeated enemies by castrating them and their children and selling them into slavery.

6   A reference to, *"Say to the believing women that they should lower their eyes and guard their private parts and not display their adornments – except for what normally shows – and draw their head-coverings across their breasts. They should not display*

their adornments except to their husbands or their fathers or their husbands' fathers, or their sons or their husbands' sons or their brothers or their brothers' sons or their sisters' sons or other women or those they own as slaves or their male attendants who have no sexual desire or children who still have no awareness of women's private parts." Surat an-Nur, 31.

7   A village near Madinah

8   Allah also 'veils' in the sense of veiling our wrong actions, and if we ask Him He will veil them on the Last Day. Note also that *"ghafara* – He forgave" means that "He covered over" the wrong action so that the slave does not see it in his reckoning on the Last Day. This applies to those wrong actions pertaining to rights due to Allah. As for wrong actions pertaining to rights due to people, those must be redressed and/or pardon sought of the person, since otherwise he or she may demand them of the one who wronged them on the Last Day. And it is said that if one is unable to redress that wrong, one must du'a for that person as much as possible.

9   A hadith with the same import is narrated by an-Nasa'i.

10   *"Prohibited to you are your mothers, your daughters, your sisters, your maternal aunts and your paternal aunts, your brothers' daughters and your sisters' daughters, your foster mothers who have suckled you, your foster sisters by suckling, your wives' mothers, your stepdaughters who are under your protection: the daughters of your wives with whom you have had sexual relations – though if you have not had sexual relations with them there is nothing blameworthy for you in it then – the wives of your sons whom you have fathered, and marrying two sisters at the same time – except for what already happened in the past. Allah is All-Forgiving, Most Merciful."* Surat an-Nisa', 23.

CHAPTER 13

1   *Sunan Abu Dawud* and *Jami' at-Tirmidhi.*

2   Malik in the *Muwatta'*, *Sahih al-Bukhari*, *Sahih Muslim*, *Jami' at-Tirmidhi*, *Sunan Ibn Majah* and ad-Darimi.

3   Malik in the *Muwatta'*, *Sahih al-Bukhari*, *Jami' at-Tirmidhi*, ad-Darimi and *Musnad Ahmad*.

4   *Sahih al-Bukhari*, *Jami' at-Tirmidhi* and *Sunan Abu Dawud*.

5   Shu'bah said that this exception is the words of Ibn 'Umar.

6   Meaning ostentatiously as if it is a part of the Sunnah, and not just washing dirt off the hands.

7   *Sahih al-Bukhari*, *Sahih Muslim* and *Musnad Ahmad*.

CHAPTER 14

1   *Sunan Abu Dawud*, *Jami' at-Tirmidhi*, *Sunan an-Nasa'i* and *Musnad Ahmad*.

2   The *izar* – sometimes called a waistwrapper – is a single piece of cloth wrapped around the lower half of the body much in the style of traditional Yemeni, Malay and Indonesian dress.

3   The hadith is narrated by Malik in the *Muwatta'*, al-Bukhari, Muslim, at-Tirmidhi, and Ahmad.

4   Malik in the *Muwatta'*, *Sunan Abu Dawud*, and *Musnad Ahmad*.

5   *Ishtimal as-samma'* – wearing only a garment made of a single piece of cloth without openings for the hands to emerge so that when the wearer brings out his hands from beneath the garment he exposes his private parts.

6   Wool is 'suf' in Arabic. Among the early Muslims those who did-without the world often wore rough wool because it was the cheapest of materials. However, it was already the case that some people wanted to be known for their doing-without, of which wool garments had become an outward sign.

7   This last from the *Muwatta'*.

8 *Qalanis* – caps, the singular of which is *qalansuwah, qulansiyah, qalsuwah* and *qalsah*. They are sometimes worn beneath turbans and sometimes alone. At some points Muslims wore tall pointed ones. The Companions wore caps which were close to the head. The Fez or tarbush is a recent example which was worn all over the Muslim world and in its time was a clear symbol of the unity of the Muslim community.

9 Al-Yarmuk was the battle in Sham fought against the Romans in 13 AH.

10 *Mahamil* – comprising two large panniers which hung on either side of the camel, containing equal loads and thus helping to balance each other and completed with the *Hawdaj* tent over them

11 *Jami' at-Tirmidhi*

12 Ibn Farhun said, "Someone asked him about that and he said, 'I thought about a people *"…who said, 'Allah is enough for us and an excellent guardian.' So they returned with a blessing from Allah and bounty and evil did not touch them. They followed the good pleasure of Allah, and Allah is Possessor of tremendous bounty"* Surah Ali 'Imran, 173-174.'"

13 It is possible that the prohibition here is because of the possibility of usury entering into a transaction involving the item with the small amount of gold in it.

14 *Ghaliyah* – a compound of musk, ambergris, camphor and oil of ben which are cooked together.

15 Malik in the *Muwatta', Sahih al-Bukhari.*

CHAPTER 15

1 Part of a hadith narrated by Malik in *Muwatta',* and confirmed by a hadith in *Sahih al-Bukhari.*

2 *Kharazah* – see the entry in Lane's Lexicon for more on this ancient form of

magic involving the wearing of single gems or beads for magical purposes.

3   In the first edition, it was mistakenly translated as a mouth ulcer, but *qarhah* refers to any wound, lesion or ulcer on the surface of the skin.

4   See the hadith in *Sahih al-Bukhari* on the use of camel's urine for medicinal treatment.

5   *"And He sent down for you of grazing livestock eight in pairs."* Surat az-Zumar, 6. The eight types of grazing livestock are the male and female of camels, cattle, sheep and goats.

6   See Surah 113, al-Falaq and the reasons for its revelation, which is that the Jew Labid ibn al-Asamm and his daughters put a spell on the Prophet ﷺ by tying knots in a string and spitting over it.

7   The Seal of Solomon is also the six-pointed star of modern zionism. The Jews slandered Sulayman ﷺ by their claim that he was a magician. The mediaeval reputation of the Jews was for two things: magic and usury. In Europe the Cabbala was reputed to be a great book of magic, falsely claimed to be the magical tradition of the Prophets, particularly Musa and Sulayman, peace be upon them. Much of this material was later incorporated into freemasonry.

8   *Nafatha* means to blow with a little spittle, so that it is less than spitting but more than blowing.

9   *Sahih al-Bukhari*.

10   Malik in the *Muwatta'*.

11   *Humrah* – literally 'redness' – a disease which causes an inflammation.

12   I have been unable to find out to what this refers – Trans.

13   The story is in the *Muwatta'*.

14   A superstition.

15 Safar is the month after Muharram. It was forbidden to fight in Muharram. Sometimes before Islam the Arabs allowed fighting in that month, and then forbade it in Safar. Malik regarded this as the reference here. Others interpret it as referring to the superstition that hunger is a snake or a reptile in the belly and that it is contagious.

16 From *Sahih al-Bukhari* and *Musnad Ahmad*.

17 Abu Dawud narrated it and al-Hakim declared it *sahih* from Anas. It is in the *Muwatta'* that a woman came to the Prophet ﷺ and he said the above quoted words to her. Misfortune can be a result of wrong actions. Perhaps the saying of the Prophet ﷺ was an allusion to that, thus dispelling the superstitious idea that the house itself was unlucky.

18 Malik in the *Muwatta'*, *Sahih Muslim*, *Jami' at-Tirmidhi* and *Sunan Ibn Majah*.

19 When the Prophet ﷺ conquered Khaybar, the Jewess Zaynab bint al-Harith, who was the wife of Salam ibn Mishkam, prepared a roasted sheep for the Prophet and his Companions which she poisoned. He began to taste a portion of it and then spat it out and said, "This bone has told me that it is poisoned." *Sirah Ibn Hisham*.

20 Malik in the *Muwatta'* and *Sahih al-Bukhari*.

CHAPTER 16

1   This question was not put out of disrespect for the above-mentioned hadith, but seeking clarification of the ruling on it.

2   i.e. it comes under the ruling that dogs must be for animal husbandry or agriculture.

3   There is unanimous agreement that it is forbidden to castrate a human being. See *al-Fawakih ad-Dawani* 376/2.

4   The Messenger ﷺ said, "In Madinah there are jinn which have accepted

Islam. If you see any of them then warn it for three days. If it appears to you after that, then kill it, for it is a shaytan." Malik in the *Muwatta'*.

5   See the hadith of 'Aishah ❀ related by Ahmad.

6   Sa'id ibn al-Musayyab narrated from 'Abd ar-Rahman ibn 'Uthman that he said, "A doctor mentioned a remedy to the Messenger of Allah ❀ and that frogs are used in it and the Messenger of Allah ❀ prohibited killing frogs." *Musnad Ahmad, Sunan Abu Dawud* and *Sunan Ibn Majah*.

CHAPTER 17

1   Slavery is neither instituted by Islam nor abolished by it, nor has our age got rid of it, but rather has substituted institutionalised refugee camps, permanent unemployment for huge numbers of people and prostitution on an unimaginable scale for what within Islam was a merciful familial arrangement and from which ex-slaves easily rose by the powers of their talents to the uppermost echelons of Muslim society. Moreover, comparison of the terms of modern employment contracts with the shari'ah might well show them to be concealed forms of slavery, rather than agreements entered into and negotiated by two free parties.

2   *Sahih al-Bukhari*.

3   Malik in *Muwatta'*.

4   Surah Yusuf, 25. She was Zulaykha and her 'master' was her husband, al-'Aziz

5   "*The angels called him while he was standing in prayer in the Upper Room: 'Allah gives you good news of Yahya, confirming a Word from Allah, and a master (Sayyid) and one who is chaste, a Prophet and one of the right-acting'.*" Surah Ali 'Imran, 39

6   There are a number of hadiths narrated in *Sahih Muslim* discountenancing

a slave's use of the word '*rabb* – lord' for his master, since that is used for Allah, exalted is He, but suggesting instead "*sayyidi*, or *mawlaya* – my master'. Similarly, masters are urged not to use the term "*abdi* – my slave' but instead terms like '*ghulami* – my boy', or '*fataya* – my young man', etc.

7   *Sahih al-Bukhari, Sunan Ibn Majah*, ad-Darimi and *Musnad Ahmad.*

8   Malik in the *Muwatta'*

9   *Sahih al-Bukhari.* It is No.15 of the Forty Hadith of Imam an-Nawawi. See the commentary on it and on the other hadiths in *The Complete Forty Hadith*, Ta-Ha Publishing, London, 1998.

10 *Sahih al-Bukhari.*

11 He 🌸 indicated with his index finger and the middle finger. At-Tirmidhi narrated the hadith and said that it is *hasan sahih*.

12 Corroborated by the hadith narrated by Ibn 'Umar 🌸 that the Messenger 🌸 "The house which is most beloved to Allah is the house in which there is an orphan who is honoured generously."

13 Muslim narrated a similar hadith with some difference in wording.

14 "*The ones who, when an affliction strikes them, say, 'We belong to Allah and we return to Him.' Those are the ones who will have blessings and mercy from their Lord; those are the guided.*" Surat al-Baqarah, 155-6.

15 *Sahih al-Bukhari, Sahih Muslim* and *Jami' at-Tirmidhi.*

16 The hadith is also narrated by Muslim but with some differences.

17 The 'oath' referred to is, "*There is not one of you who will not come to it (the Fire).*" (Surah Maryam, 71)

18 "*And then when he attained his ashudd, We granted him judgement and knowledge. That is how We recompense good-doers.*" (Surah Yusuf, 22)

CHAPTER 18

1   Substantially the same as a hadith of Abu Hurayrah in *Sahih al-Bukhari*.

2   "One mounted person is a shaytan, two mounted people are two shaytans, and three are a mounted party." *Musnad Ahmad*.

3   Malik in the *Muwatta'*.

4   In *Sahih Muslim* some say "three days".

5   Possibly meaning that it invalidates his standing as someone whose testimony would be accepted.

CHAPTER 19

1   Al-Bukhari, Muslim, Ibn Majah and Ahmad narrate this hadith in other forms.

2   Confirmed by a hadith in *Sahih al-Bukhari*.

3   Al-Bukhari narrates the hadith almost identically from Abu Qatadah.

4   'Aishah ﷺ dreamt that three moons fell into her house. She told her father and he did not interpret the dream, until after the death of the Prophet ﷺ.

CHAPTER 20

1   Some people imagine the strictures on music apply equally to the mass-market music of our age, the symphonies of Beethoven, and the Diwans of the Sufis. If one examines these three forms – and there are others which would represent different cases in fiqh – in each case the intention behind the music is different, the content is different, and the intentions of performers and audience are different.

2   Usually attributed to Labid.

3   Al-Bukhari in *al-Adab*, al-Baihaqi in *as-Sunan* and at-Tabarani in *al-Kabir*.

4   *Sunan Abu Dawud*.

5   Literally 'hoofed' creatures.

6   Literally 'padded' creatures.

7   A word signifying weapons with sharp heads.

8   A third rider in the contest who does not place a wager but who, if he wins, takes the stakes of the other two riders.

9   i.e. the Sultan or Amir.

10 *Musalli* is the same word as for the 'one who performs salat'.

CHAPTER 21

1   "*Permission to fight is given to those who are fought against because they have been wronged – truly Allah is able to help them – those who were expelled from their homes unrightfully, merely for saying, 'Our Lord is Allah.' If Allah had not driven some people back by means of others, monasteries, churches, synagogues and mosques, where Allah's name is mentioned much, would have been pulled down and destroyed. Allah will certainly help those who help Him. Allah is All-Strong, Almighty. Those who, if We establish them firmly on the earth, they establish the prayer and pay Zakat, and command the right and forbid the wrong. The end result of all affairs is with Allah.*" Surat al-Hajj, 37-39.

2   Fitnah here has also been interpreted as 'idolatry'.

3   The Ansar came to al-'Aqabah three times. Twelve came the second time and pledged allegiance without the condition of fighting in what is known as 'The Pledge of Allegiance of Women'. The third time a substantially greater body of people came, numbering some seventy or more, and they pledged allegiance with the explicit understanding that they would fight to defend the Messenger ﷺ. See the *Sirah* of Ibn Hisham.

4   He was not a Muslim, but Abu Bakr chose him as a guide for the journey.

5   A reference to the ayat of Qur'an, "*A mosque which is founded upon fear of*

Allah from the first day has more right that you should stand for prayer in it." Surat at-Tawbah, 108.

6 Also known as Waddan. It was the first expedition.

7 Safwan is in the region of Badr and so this expedition is known as the First Badr.

8 "*They ask you about the sacred month, about fighting in it. Say, 'Fighting in it is serious but preventing people from the way of Allah, and disbelieving in Him, and preventing people from the Sacred Mosque and expelling its people from it is more serious with Allah. And the oppression of idolatry is more serious than killing'.*" Surat al-Baqarah, 217.

9 *Shuhada'* sing. *shaheed* means 'martyrs', because the English word in its root also signifies 'witness' as does the Arabic word. However, since the English word has come to signify passive suffering and the vicarious cruel thrill of onlookers, we have abandoned its use as the translation of *shaheed*. The *shaheed* who is killed fighting in the Way of Allah goes joyously to his Lord in the Garden without awaiting the resurrection and the accounting in the grave.

10 *Saweeq* is a meal of parched barley.

11 Also known as the raid on Ghatafan.

12 A reference to "*...those who responded to Allah and the Messenger after the wound had been inflicted will have a huge reward.*" Surah Al 'Imran, 172. The effect of this raid was to convince the kuffar that the Muslims had suffered less from Uhud than they really had and it deterred them from attacking Madinah.

13 A place in the lands of Hudhayl. The battle took place close to it.

14 They asked the Messenger ﷺ to expel them without shedding their blood

on the basis that they could have what their camels could carry except for their weapons, and he agreed to that. Surat al-Hashr was revealed about this event.

15 The ayah by which it was revealed was Surat an-Nisa, 102.

16 It was called the Trench because the Muslims dug a trench in the stretch between mountains where Madinah is undefended. This was on the advice of Salman al-Farsi who had experienced such methods of warfare in Persia. However, the kuffar were completely unprepared for such an eventuality. They encamped for a while and then, irritated by a wind which blew for days, went home.

17 It was named the 'Confederates' because of the uniting of a number of groups of the kuffar, i.e. Quraysh, Ghatafan and, treacherously, the Jews of Madinah who were in a treaty with the Prophet 鵜.

18 Bani Quraydhah were the Jewish tribe who treacherously allied themselves with the kuffar. When the Messenger of Allah 鵜 returned to Madinah after the siege of the Trench and the Muslims had put down their weapons, Jibril 鵜 came to the Messenger with the command that he should go against Bani Quraydhah. The crier of the Messenger announced that no one should pray Salat al-'Asr except at Bani Quraydhah. When the siege became severe they surrendered. The Prophet 鵜 appointed their ally, Sa'd ibn Mu'adh, to pass judgement on them. He judged that they should be offered Islam which if they accepted they should be forgiven and live, but that otherwise the men were to be beheaded, the women and children enslaved, and their property divided up.

19 There were three hundred Muslims on this raid, during which their provisions were exhausted so that they were reduced to eating one date a

day. Then they came to the coast where they found a great fish, probably a whale. So they stayed there eating from it for eighteen days.

The Prophet ﷺ said about the sea, "It's water is pure, and its dead creatures are halal," i.e. those creatures which have not been slaughtered by Muslims but have died in some other manner.

The raid had been against a caravan of Quraysh and to raid a subsection of the tribe of Juhaynah close to the coast who lived at a distance of five days journey from Madinah.

20 This raid came about in Rabi' al-Awwal. The Messenger ﷺ came to know that a group were gathering there.

21 There are a number of Companions with this name.

22 Ghalib ibn 'Abdillah is said to have travelled with sixty cavalry and to have killed some kuffar and driven off their cattle. At the Opening of Makkah, he was the man whom the Messenger of Allah ﷺ chose to go before him to ease the way.

23 Baliy is an area of the Yemen.

24 Al-Juhfah is the place six miles from the coast which is the *miqat* for the people of Syria. i.e. it is there that people performing the Hajj or the 'Umrah must don *ihram*.

25 Specifically in Surat an-Nur, 11. However, a great deal of Surat an-Nur revolves around this story.

26 So called because Allah, mighty is He and majestic, revealed His being pleased with those who swore allegiance under the Tree at al-Hudaybiyyah that day: *"Allah was pleased with the believers when they swore allegiance to you under the Tree. He knew what was in their hearts and sent down tranquillity upon them and has rewarded them with an imminent victory."* Surat al-Fath, 19.

27 Khaybar in the language of the Jews means a fortress. Khaybar was well
known for having many date-palms. It lay almost one hundred miles from
Madinah. The Messenger 🙵 went to it in Muharram and conquered it
by force, then made a treaty with them allowing them to remain on their
land for payment of half the crop. He said to them, "I allow you to remain
as long as Allah allows you to remain." In the khalifate of 'Umar they
became openly promiscuous and made jokes about the Muslims. When
'Umar learnt of the hadith of the Prophet 🙵 that two deens were not to
coexist in the Arabian Peninsula, he expelled them to Syria.

28 Ka'b ibn 'Umayr al-Ghifari. They were a group of fifteen men.

29 Possibly Dhat Islah.

30 Some count it as one of the districts of Madinah. Others say that it is seven
days journey from Damascus, in between it and Madinah.

31 A town two days' journey from Madinah and less than a day's journey
from Khaybar.

32 A *waqf* (pl. *awqaf*) is an endowment of property devoted to some purpose.
Some, but not all, *awqaf* yield an income. They can be devoted to the
upkeep of relatives, one's descendants or for a charitable purpose. A great
deal of the fabric of Muslim society was sustained by the *awqaf* system for
centuries.

33 A reference to the words of Allah, exalted is He, "*Whatever booty from them
Allah has given to His Messenger, you did not hurry on either horse or camel for it.*"
Surat al-Hashr, 6.

34 Wadi al-Qura is a valley between Madinah and Syria in which there were
many small villages (*qura*).

35 Heraclius, the Roman Emperor in Constantinople. The Muslim sources

speak of his accepting the truth of the mission of the Prophet ﷺ but of his fearing his generals so much that he kept his belief secret.

36 See *Sahih al-Bukhari*, "The Book of the Beginning of Revelation."

37 i.e. they had prevented him in the year of al-Hudaybiyyah. So he went out in the same month to perform the *'umrah* which he had intended to do that time. Therefore it is called *'Umrat al-Qada* – the *'umrah* to be performed in place of the one missed. He went out six days before the end of Dhu'l-Qa'dah.

38 A place eight miles from Makkah.

39 Sarif is a place approximately six miles from Makkah.

40 Mentioned in *Sahih al-Bukhari*. See also Qadi 'Iyad's treatment of this matter in *ash-Shifa*, published as *Muhammad the Messenger of Allah* by Diwan Press.

41 Ja'far ibn Abi Talib, 'Ali's brother and the cousin of the Prophet ﷺ.

42 *Fath* means 'opening [to Islam]' rather than conquest.

43 It is usually considered that some allies of Quraysh had broken the truce by killing allies of the Muslims, and Abu Sufyan was trying to avert the obvious consequence which was the invalidation of the treaty.

44 An oasis belonging to Bani Judhaymah who resided in lower Makkah a night's journey away in the direction of Yalamlam.

45 A reference to the ayah of Qur'an: *"So watch for a day when the sky produce a clear smoke which will envelop people. This is a painful punishment."* Surat ad-Dukhan, 10-11. There are many interpretations of this ayah, one of which is that it is the famine which happened to Quraysh because of the supplication of the Messenger ﷺ. It became so severe that a man would see what appeared to be smoke between the sky and the earth. Another famous interpretation is that it refers to events before the end of time.

46 Hunayn is a valley three nights' journey from Makkah, to the side of Dhu'l-Majaz and near to at-Ta'if. It is between thirteen and nineteen miles away in the same direction as 'Arafat. The battle is referred to in Surat at-Tawbah, 25-27. The Muslims felt supremely confident since they had just opened Makkah to Islam, and had an enormous army of ten thousand Madinans and two thousand Makkans. Hawazin launched a surprise attack and it was only because the Prophet ☀ held his ground and a few men with him and rallied the Muslims that a defeat turned into victory.

47 However, Allah, exalted is He had not granted him ☀ to conquer at-Ta'if at this time and they lifted the siege.

48 Tabuk was the nearest part of Syria to the Muslims. It is between Wadi al-Qura and Syria.

49 They were Ka'b ibn Malik, Murarah ibn ar-Rabi' al-'Amiri and Hilal ibn Umayyah al-Waqidi. All of them were true Muslims who allowed themselves to become distracted. As on other occasions the hypocrites had prepared excuses and the Messenger of Allah ☀, who judged by the shari'ah and not by any knowledge he may have had of their state, pardoned them. However, the three Muslims told the truth about their failure to come on the expedition. They were shunned and no one spoke to them for fifty days until Allah revealed their forgiveness in Surat at-Tawbah, 118. The whole story is told at length by Ka'b ibn Malik in Ibn Hisham's *Sirah* and in the works of hadith.

50 The opening of the Surah proclaims that idolaters are no longer to perform the Hajj, and it allowed them four months in which to accept Islam.

51 Tulayhah had claimed to be a prophet.

52 See his biography in the appendix. It is a measure of his immensity as

a man of knowledge that Ibn Abi Zayd should choose to conclude this section with mention of his birth.

www.ingramcontent.com/pod-product-compliance
Lightning Source LLC
Chambersburg PA
CBHW031246090426
42742CB00007B/335